P9-DCV-167

THE ORCHARD MASON BEE

THE ORCHARD MASON BEE

(Osmia lignaria propinqua Cresson)

The Life History,
Biology, Propagation, and Use
of a
North American
Native Bee

by
BRIAN L. GRIFFIN
illustrated by Sharon Smith, and the author

2nd Edition
1999

Knox Cellars Publishing, Bellingham, WA

Second Edition 1999

Knox Cellars Publishing, Bellingham, Washington USA
E-mail: brian@knoxcellars.com
Website: http://www.knoxcellars.com

Copyright@1999 by Brian L. Griffin

Copyright. All rights reserved under International and Pan American Conventions

No part of this book may be reproduced or transmitted in any form or by any means (electronic, photocopying, recording or otherwise) without the prior written permission of the author, Brian L. Griffin, 1607 Knox Ave., Bellingham, WA 98225. Published in the United States by Knox Cellars Publishing, Bellingham, Washington

Library of Congress Cataloging-in-Publication Data pending

Griffin, Brian L.

Includes bibliographical references

Cover painting by Brian L. Griffin
Design/Composition: Kathleen R. Weisel

ISBN: number 0-9635841-2-X

Printed in the United States of America

Acknowledgements

The author expresses his gratitude to the following:

Dr. Philip F. Torchio, retired from the U.S.D.A Bee Biology Laboratory, Utah State University, for his ongoing generosity in supplying invaluable technical information. At the time of the first edition of this book he unselfishly supplied copies of numerous scientific papers written by himself and others, describing studies of *Osmia lignaria*. He also read that original manuscript for errors in fact. Over the years he has responded to numerous questions from the author in personal correspondence and conversations. His science and his friendship are appreciated.

Beverly Johanson, a good friend and English teacher, who for the third time has edited my literary efforts making an embarrassing number of corrections and criticisms.

My cousin, and friend, Marc Miller, who sent to me the Washington State University Extension Service Bulletin which introduced me to the Orchard Mason Bee.

Marya Griffin, my wife and gardening partner, who still supports and endures the time and energy that my bee activities consume.

Dedication

To my parents
Earle and Alma Griffin

Who throughout their lives encouraged
by example and deed my active interest in the
natural world. I dedicate this little book
to their memory.

 # Contents

About the Author

Brian Griffin, a graduate of Whitman College with a degree in English literature, was born in Bellingham, Washington in 1932. A childhood spent exploring the tide pools and forests of the San Juan Islands whetted his curiosity about natural things. Years spent afield hiking and hunting sharpened his powers of observation, and, finally, an inspiring natural history teacher at Whitman College, Arthur Rempel, focused his interest and fueled his curiosity further.

Griffin has spent a long career in business, but has always found time to observe and enjoy nature. For the past 12 years he has propagated Orchard Mason Bees. This book is a recitation of his experiences with and study of the Orchard Mason Bee.

He has written a second book about native bees *Humblebee Bumblebee* and is working on a third book about the art and practice of growing fruit trees in the espalier method. He and his daughter Lisa Novich, are extremely busy with their business— Knox Cellars Native Bee Pollinators—selling Orchard Mason Bees, and native bee related items.

About the Illustrator

Sharon Smith has been observing and drawing nature for more than 26 years. She graduated from the University of California at Santa Barbara, majoring in Biology and Art, and is a member of the Guild of Natural Science Illustrators.

Sharon's love of nature and rural life brought her to the Pacific Northwest, where she lives deep in the woods beside the Nooksack River.

Previously, she has illustrated children's picture books, a tide pool guidebook, and taken private commissions.

Preface

I would never have guessed during the late spring of 1993, that the little book I was writing, *The Orchard Mason Bee*, would, in a period of six years, launch a small industry, sell almost sixteen thousand copies, and lead me into a new career which now threatens to consume my retirement. Now in the early spring of 1999, I find myself beginning a second edition, driven by the need to include in the book the new knowledge that I have accumulated during these years about that gentle spring pollinator, the Orchard Mason bee.

The story of my introduction to the Orchard Mason Bee and the progression from raising them for backyard pollination to the development of the present business of selling bees, books and nesting materials to gardeners in every state of the Union is an entrepreneurial story that my readers might enjoy.

It all began in my back yard in Bellingham, Washington, a small city of seventy thousand people in the very northwest corner of the United States. For many springs I had seen them, small black insects feeding on my flowering shrubs. Sometimes I wondered what they were. Mostly I gave them little notice and soon forgot about them. When the blossom time passed they were forgotten until they reappeared the next spring.

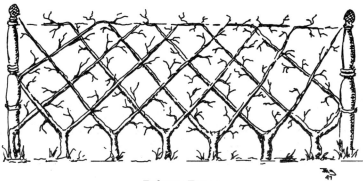

Belgian Fence

Then one year I planted a Belgian Fence, a long fence consisting of forty fruit trees, trained in the espalier method. Two trees each of twenty varieties of apples and pears growing in a formal grid pattern along the lower side of our back yard. The problems of urban pollination soon made themselves known.

The fruit trees grew nicely; each spring they burst forth with more and more blossoms, but the fruit yield was always disappointing. There simply were not enough honeybees working on those cold spring days to pollinate the trees.

A friend, hearing of my troubles, sent me Washington State University Extension Service Bulletin #0922, *Orchard Mason Bees*, and a fascinating door opened for me.

I read the bulletin and immediately realized that the black insects I had seen each spring were indeed a small native population of Orchard Mason Bees that had been nesting in the wooden shingle roof of our garden shed.

Following the bulletin's instructions, I drilled a number of holes in a fir 4 × 6, hung it on the southerly wall of the garden house and watched expectantly. The very next day I began to notice little black bees going in and out of the drilled holes.

My adventure with *Osmia lignaria propinqua* Cresson had begun. Soon every hole in the wooden block was sealed with a grey mud plug. I drilled another block and hung it on the garden shed. I had eighty-five filled holes that first year. Each hole contained about five nesting cells. I had collected about five hundred bees.

The next spring the population of bees on the big *Pieris japonica* (*Andromeda japonica*) shrub next to the garden house was much larger. When the apples and pears blossomed I frequently saw my little black friends working the Belgian fence

By the first of June that year I had 583 filled nesting holes, a 680% increase in bees. I also had a vastly improved fruit set and a fine crop of apples and pears. Each year since then the fruit harvest has been generous. The bees thrive on the garden house wall, and the offspring of my original bee population has been spreading fruitfulness in urban and rural gardens throughout the United States.

One December morning, in that third year, filled with the holiday spirit, I was wondering what I might make in my workshop to give to friends as a Christmas gift. It dawned on me that others might find wonder in the spring activities of the Orchard Mason Bee. Inspired with creative energy, I rushed to my workshop. There I fashioned a little wooden block into the shape of a peak roofed house, drilled a dozen nesting holes into it, applied an over-hanging roof, and then, heart in mouth, sliced from one of my many bee-filled nesting blocks, a three-hole slice containing hibernating bees. I was able to make this delicate cut without slicing into the nesting holes and I now had a nicely pro-

The Pollinator

portioned, thin slice of wood containing three nesting holes and about fifteen bees. Hopefully they were undisturbed by the saw blade and still deep in their hibernation sleep. I carefully nailed the slice of bees to the bottom of the "bee house."

Now my little gift lacked only instructions and an indication of what it was. With a wood burner I inscribed **"Orchard Mason Bees"** in the peak under the roof, and then typed some instructions and a bit of an explanation on brown paper which I fashioned into a hang tag attached with a thread under the roof. The idea which would launch a business was born.

I gave twenty of these little houses that I had dubbed "pollinators" to friends and relatives that Christmas. They were received with great interest, truly a unique and different gift. The real pleasure came the following spring when every one of the "pollinators" burst forth with their awakening bees, and the twelve empty holes of the little houses were filled with nest cells by the hard working bees.

My friends were fascinated. My idea had been a success.

By the fourth year my bee population hibernating in wooden nesting blocks stacked in my unheated garage was huge. I had many more bees than I needed. Then another idea formed. Perhaps the little "pollinator" was a salable item. I called on Marcy Plattner, a friend who owns The Garden Spot Nursery in my home town of Bellingham, and who had contracted for a large double booth at the Northwest Flower & Garden Show at Seattle's convention center. Marcy was kind enough to let me use a tiny corner of her booth in return for a modest share of whatever my sales might be. I went to that February 1992 Garden Show armed with boxes of "pollinators," a brief printed handout, and abundant enthusiasm. I was astonished at the results. Of the hundreds of people that I talked with during the five days of the show, only two had heard of the bee and yet I sold over two hundred "pollinators." People found the concept intriguing. I now knew there was a market for pollinating bees.

That spring and summer I wrote the first edition of *The Orchard Mason Bee*, deciding to publish and market it myself. Before long I found myself making and selling large nesting blocks without bees for those people with expanding bee populations. Each year the Seattle garden show demonstrated the growing awareness and acceptance of the bee and my expanding line of bee products, several national magazines and catalog companies took note, writing articles and selling some of my bee products.

Suddenly pollination by bees was in the news.

Honeybee populations in North America were under siege. Two species of foreign mites had invaded the continent and were rapidly decimating both feral and managed honeybee populations as they spread north from their point of entry in South America. The mites had been accidental riders on queen honeybees imported from the Old World. The blood sucking varroa mite and the equally lethal tracheal mite spread inexorably northward until, by 1997, they occupied the entire continental United States. As a result, the nation's feral honeybee population had been reduced an estimated ninety percent. Commercial beekeepers, medicating their hives with miticides were losing an alarming percentage of their hives each winter and barely holding their own against the scourge. Suddenly North America faced a pollination crisis which has shown no measure of improvement to the date of this writing.

Entomologists such as the USDA's Philip Torchio, who, for years, had been championing the cause of our continent's native bees, now began to be heard. The national press began to take notice, national gardening magazines published many articles telling the public about the importance of our native bees, and the Orchard Mason surely got its share of the press. The honeybee's troubles proved a great business builder for me. Fortunately the mites that decimate the honey bee population do not prey on any of North Americas native bees.

I got so busy with the bees that I soon enlisted the aid of one of my daughters, Lisa Griffin Novich. Lisa had left her job in industry several years earlier to answer the call of being an at-home mother to her three young children. As her children reached school age, Lisa was ready for a challenge. She proved to be a natural fit in the bee business and soon she became a full partner in what now has become a full time job for both of us.

What began with a planting of fruit trees in the back yard has become a small industry — both manufacturing a range of native bee products and selling the bees themselves. Our products are sold wholesale and retail, from store shelves and over the Internet. This activity has become a second career that provides great joy and satisfaction to the author.

It is my earnest hope that you will find my story of the Orchard Mason Bee interesting. If this book does its job, you will soon be out shopping for nesting habitat or in the garage with an electric drill preparing for next spring's blossom time. You will find this gentle little bee fun to watch and fruitful to encourage.

If you are lucky enough to have a native population to develop as I did, this book will provide you with all that you need to propagate your own pollinators. If you don't have the Orchard Mason where you live, you can buy a "starter set" of bees from one of the retail stores that carry our products, or directly from Knox Cellars.

Chapter 1

The Friendly Pollinator

Washington State University gave our little friend its name; Orchard Mason Bee. The true scientific name is *Osmia lignaria propinqua* Cresson. In much of the country it is known as the Blue Orchard Bee. We will call it the Orchard Mason Bee in our book out of respect for that extension service which first brought it to our consciousness, and because Orchard Mason nicely describes both its lifestyle and its beneficial nature.

Osmia lignaria belongs to the insect order *Hymenoptera* that includes the ants, bees and wasps. To further isolate its classification, it belongs to the family *Megachilidae*, which in Latin means thick-jawed bees. Of course, we have already reported its genus, *Osmia*, its species, *Lignaria*, and its subspecies, *propinqua*. All of the *megachilid*s are considered long-tongued bees (better to collect nectar from flowers).

The Orchard Mason Bee is native to the United States and Canada west of the Rocky Mountains. Its eastern cousin, *Osmia lignaria lignaria* Say, populates most of North America east of the Rockies. Only Florida and two of its neighbor states do not have a native population of Orchard Masons, but even there the bees can be successfully propagated by refrigerating them in the winter months thereby simulating a northern winter.

The cousins are virtually identical except for a different set to the female's two facial horns used in shaping the mud masonry in their nesting chambers. The western bee has horns that project horizontally from the bee's face, while the horns of the eastern bee project downward at about a forty-five-degree angle. Science has been unable to discover any other difference. If transported across their prehistoric mountain barrier, each subspecies does well in the other's ancestral territory. They interbreed readily.

You can easily find the Orchard Mason by looking on flowering shrubs and fruit trees early in the spring and by watching for black insects investigating holes and cracks in buildings or trees. In coastal northwest Washington State where we live, the *Pieris japonica (Andromeda japonica)* shrub is among the first of the domestic plants to blossom and is an excellent place to look for the first of the emerging bees. In this climate *Pieris* always blooms by mid-February, long before the bees emerge, and as I write on

May 6th, the plant is still in a dwindling bloom and still attracting the bees. Many insects flock to its fragrant flowers to gather the energy they will need for their annual mission.

In your own locale watch for the earliest of your native blooms. They will most likely herald the emergence of the Orchard Mason Bee. In the Pacific Northwest the reliable indicator is the native Oregon grape. Its bright yellow blooms signal the beginning of bee emergence. In the foothills of the Wasatch Mountains in Utah the purplish hydrophylum that carpets the canyons and washes at the lower mountain levels each spring indicates bee season and supports a large population of *Osmia lignaria.*

Wander the woods and byways of your part of North America in the early spring and observe the early blooms. There you will find the earliest of the pollinators and among them, the Orchard Mason Bees fueling themselves with energy-laden nectar. Nature has linked the time of the bees to the blossoms.

Our tiny friend is shiny black. Seen in bright sunlight you might call it shiny blue-black. Perhaps it is black because it emerges in the very early cool spring; it must absorb heat from what sun there is at that time of the year for a bee cannot fly until its body temperature reaches about fifty-five degrees Fahrenheit. You will often see Orchard Masons sunning themselves on cool clear days. Even though the ambient temperature might be well below fifty-five degrees Fahrenheit, the bees can function as long as they can stay in the sun, absorbing its warmth into their dark bodies. If a cloud passes over the warming sun and the bee cools down, it must land and may be stranded far from home too cold to return.

Many people, when seeing their first Orchard Mason exclaim, "Why it looks just like a fly." It is small, winged and black but there the resemblance ends. Like all bees, it has four wings (flies have but two). The bees have antennae; flies do not. Bees at rest fold their wings close to their bodies; flies rest with their wings in a modified V shape somewhat reminiscent of a stealth bomber.

Most likely the first Orchard Mason that you see in the spring will be a male. He is smaller than the female and is distinguished from her by a white hair patch on his face. The male has long antennae that sweep back in a graceful curve. The female is completely black. Her antennae are about half as long as the male's. Many females are as large or larger than honeybees. They are rather chunky and robust looking and have slightly flattened abdomens.

You will notice significant differences in the size of bees in a season, as well as difference in bee size from year to year. The size of all bees is determined by the amount of food provided the larvae and so good natural conditions result in large bees. Size differences in the bees that you see in the same season might be the result of a cold spell the previous spring when the small bee's mother was gathering provisions for its egg. A larger bee might have been fortunate to have its egg laid during a warm, flower rich period that same spring.

The Orchard Mason is a solitary-gregarious bee. This seeming contradictory description means that, while they nest in groups, if there is an adequacy of nesting holes, they are indeed solitary in nesting and propagating their species. After mating they seem to

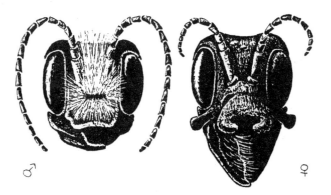

Male and female Orchard Mason Bee faces.

have no interest in one another, but like the swallows that gregariously nest at the Mission San Juan Capistrano, they all want to nest close together. We are not sure why; it is simply a fact of nature. As solitary insects, they do not have a queen. They do not tend their young and they do no tasks that benefit the other bees of their colony.

Honeybees, in contrast, are social insects. They depend on incredible social organization to raise, protect, feed, cool, heat and continue their species. Unlike the honeybee, our Orchard Mason lives a very simple life. On the day of her emergence from the nesting cell in which she has spent the winter, the female mates, sometimes with several males. For the rest of her brief life she gathers food, lays eggs, packs mud. She works entirely alone, getting no help from males, or her fellow females who are all busy with their own labors.

The males patrol the nesting site, looking for emerging females to bestow their masculine attentions upon. They take frequent trips to the neighborhood blossoms, but only for sustenance to keep their energies at full power. Their lives are even shorter than those of the females. When they have done nature's bidding, impregnating the females, they quickly die, leaving the females to work away at the continuation of the species.

In a strange way the measured lifespan of both sexes is extended by the onset of bad weather. The female is capable of laying about thirty-four eggs in her lifetime. In a normal day she will complete one cell with food, an egg and protective walls. In extremely good weather with abundant food resources, she might complete two cells. Each completed cell represents a thirty-fourth of her life's work and about that percentage of her expected remaining life. If the day dawns too cold for her to fly, and remains that cold all day, bees of both sexes simply take the day off, reducing by that day the wear and tear on their fragile bodies which eventually ends their lives. The bees just stay in their holes expending little of the energy and life force that dictates the length of their lives.

Extreme weather swings can become fatal for bees for they must be able to fly to find the lifegiving nectar. If it is too cold for too long the bees must starve to death. In prolonged cold spells the female bee is actually able to put off starvation by resorbing some of her eggs using them for standby food. Since the bee only starts with about thirty-four eggs, long cold spells in the spring can mean a smaller number of eggs laid and a reduction of bee populations for the following year.

It is wise to remember the Orchard Masons' need for the warmth of the sun when placing their nesting blocks. In most climates the nesting blocks should hang in direct sunlight for in the early spring the ability to fly to the blossoms, even for only one-half hour, may mean the difference between life and death. Warm nesting areas will result in a larger number of cells constructed, eggs laid, and a larger population of bees for the next year.

The Orchard Mason nests in pre-existing holes. It will rarely make its own. It prefers holes in wood; however, it will use holes in other materials. In the wild it searches the forests and brush patches for an unused beetle larvae hole in a dead snag, or a broken hollow stem of a woody plant. It will nest in deep fissures in the bark of trees like Ponderosa pine.

I have found the bees living in driftwood logs thrown up on the seashore by the winter storms. They occupy the tunnels in the wood dug by the marine teredos, commonly called pileworms.

Several times I have seen them nesting deep in the recesses of a birdhouse where they built up a large mud structure not unlike the nest of the mud wasp. This is the only example that I know of where they have constructed their own nesting hole. They cannot tunnel into wood or do damage to man-made structures.

Large populations of the bees can be developed only when large numbers of the proper size holes are available. In the urban setting they readily nest in the holes created by overlapping shingles or holes wherever they can find them. Fortunately they do no damage to any buildings they occupy. They are simply filling an existing hole with their nesting cells.

This specialization in nesting habitat has no doubt limited their numbers dramatically. When compared to the adaptable honeybee, which is able to build its complex society in the walls of a house, a hollow tree, or an old box discarded by man, our Orchard Mason seems rather primitive and simple.

On the other hand, the specialized nature of the Orchard Mason results in some of the attributes that make it such a perfect urban pollinator.

First and foremost, it is entirely non-aggressive. It simply will not attack either singly or en masse. I theorize that their solitary lifestyle is the explanation for their good nature. The Orchard Mason, unlike the honeybee has nothing much to protect. In the natural setting she lays her eggs in an unused beetle hole in one part of the forest and then flies elsewhere to find another hole. Survival of her species depends on dispersal of the eggs rather than defense of the queen and castle, as with the honeybee.

You can be confident that the Orchard Masons are perfectly behaved guests in your garden. You and your neighbors won't even know they are around unless you stand watching by the nesting blocks. Often I stand in the busy flight pattern in front of my nesting blocks while dozens of bees pass my head. They are busy going and coming from their nesting holes and simply ignore me.

Once in a while I will move quickly and a bee, too late to change course, will bump into my head. Undaunted and without malice, she will bounce off and resume flight around me. Ciscoe Morris, a popular Seattle radio garden show personality delights in telling his listeners about his "Teddy Bees" that he has nesting on their covered patio dining table. While they dine Ciscoe and his wife enjoy watching the bees working up close.

The female Orchard Mason is capable of a mild sting. The male is entirely harmless. I have not been stung in the fifteen years that I have raised the bee; however, I have met several people who have had the experience. They report that 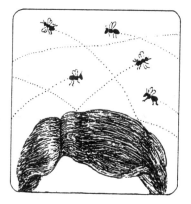 the literature is correct. The Orchard Mason sting is less troubling than a mosquito bite. The relative toxicity of the Orchard Mason's sting has apparently not been studied. In a personal communication with Dr. Philip Torchio, at the USDA Agricultural Research Service, at Utah State University, I learned that, to his knowledge, "documentation of human reactions to bee stings has been restricted to cases involving honeybees."

He cites personal knowledge of a friend who is not reactive to honeybee stings but "is highly reactive to bumblebee stings" and says, "others are highly reactive to wasp (hornet) stings but are not bothered by bee stings." He goes on to remark, "We don't really know anything about human reaction to *Osmia lignaria* stings." Surely those who are seriously allergic to insect stings and bites should be cautious in handling the Orchard Mason, however, they can take solace from the knowledge that the bee will only sting if squeezed between the fingers or caught under clothing and slapped.

Additional comfort, Torchio says, can be taken from the fact that "these bees will not attack in numbers as do honeybees or hornets when their nests are disturbed." In fact, in my experience the Orchard Mason will not attack at all, no matter how much you agitate her nesting block.

A further benefit humans derive from the specialized lifestyle of the Orchard Mason is the ease of propagating this highly effective pollinator. All the prospective beekeeper need do to develop and keep a large pollinating population in his yard is provide the bee with clean holes in which to nest and blossoms from which to dine.

Remarkably, our friendly bees are also extremely efficient pollinators. Scientific studies at Utah State University have established that they are incredibly better pollinators than the honeybee. Add to these attributes the fact that they are very easily maintained and propagated in the smallest of back yards, that they are fun and fascinating to watch, and you must conclude that Mother Nature has given us a marvelous gift to use and protect.

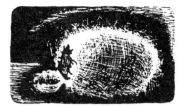

Chapter 2

Life History

Let's begin our story of the Orchard Mason's life history in the early spring, for that is when we first see them. The weather is warming; the fruit tree buds have begun to swell; the very first of the garden shrubs have just started to bloom. Somewhere, inside a cocoon, deep within a hole, the bees begin to stir.

They have spent the cold winter as fully formed adults, hibernating within the confines of a waterproof insulating cocoon. They are protected by stout mud walls constructed the previous spring by their mother. Without food or liquid they have rested there in a state of torpor, using almost no energy, just waiting for the signal of warmth. When it comes, when the temperature rises to fifty degrees Fahrenheit for a couple of days, the bees in the nesting holes awake.

The time of awakening varies from year to year, depending upon the weather. The earliest bee emergence I have observed was February twenty-seventh. More typically in Western Washington, the bees emerge in mid to late March. In colder climates emergence will be even later. In 1999, a very cool late spring, the bees in Logan, Utah had not emerged by the 15th of May.

In the typical nesting hole there will be a series of nesting chambers one after the other. They are set in the holes like bullets in the tubular magazine of a rifle. In the front, in the first seventy percent of the nesting chambers, are the males. They awaken first and begin to chew away at the softer "nipple" end of the cocoon, which almost always is pointed at the entrance hole.

When he has chewed through the cocoon, the bee is confronted by a thin mud barrier; this too falls prey to his eager jaws, and now before him is another bee in some stage of awareness.

If the bee in front is a sluggard he will get a nip or two to wake him up and get him going. Sometimes the early bird behind will simply crawl over and past a slow waker.

Finally our first awaking bee confronts the thick entrance plug. This is a mud wall constructed by his mother the previous spring. It is frequently almost 1/4-inch thick and made massively to protect the young bees from a variety of predators that would dine on them.

The entrance plug is chipped and chewed away with considerable effort, and at last our eager male bee sees daylight for the first time. He will create a small hole in the plug just large enough to squeeze through. He will then crawl out of the hole, briefly exercise and stretch his wings, and quickly fly off, drawn by what must be a demonic hunger to a waiting blossom.

At our home a huge *Pieris japonica* scrub grows ten feet from where the nesting blocks hang on the side of the garden shed. The scrub is in full bloom. It has been blooming since mid-February and now the bees flock to it. They feast on its fragrant nectar and soon return to the area of the nesting blocks, frequently warming in the spring sunshine on the shed's shingle roof. The males are awaiting the emergence of the females. They will soon begin the age-old male challenge, contesting for the females in order to pass their genes onto the next generation.

One after another the males struggle out of their cocoons through the debris of the now-penetrated mud walls, and emerge into the sunlight. Soon there is a veritable men's club sunning on the roof, and trading back and forth to the *Pieris japonica.* They are waiting, gathering their strength for the trial before them. The male emergence lasts for ten to fifteen days depending upon the daily temperature.

Three to fifteen days after the emergence of the males, the first female tentatively thrusts her antennae into the sunlight. Their emergence is also regulated by the weather. Each year seems different. In warm sunny springs, female emergence seems rapid and is complete in a relatively brief number of days.

In a cold spring, the emergence can be drawn out over more than two weeks.

She is perhaps a third larger than the patrolling males. Her antennae are short and thick, and her wings appear stunted and misshapen on her back. Actually her wings are fully shaped and mature, not stunted at all. She frequently cannot fly yet, as her wings are apt to be soft and damp from the cocoon. It may take a half hour before she can take flight, a condition no doubt decreed by Mother Nature to facilitate what happens next.

The female emerges from the hole and for a moment rests on the face of the nesting block. Immediately one of the waiting males lands upon her and grasps her tightly with his six legs. Frequently several other males will pile on until the virginal female loses her grip on the nesting block and the whole grasping, clutching group falls to the ground.

On the ground, in a brief mating ritual, the female is impregnated. She may be mated by several males before the day is out. After that day she becomes all business. Her wings dry, she takes flight, and she is no longer attractive to males nor is she interested in them.

Her only imperative now is the continuation of the species. She too flies to the *Pieris japonica* to feed. Then she is off to seek a proper nesting hole. Meanwhile, her ardent lover of yesterday is back on patrol, hoping for another tryst with an emerging virgin.

Approach the nesting area gingerly during the

mating time to avoid stepping on bees crawling on the ground. We have a concrete apron in front of the garden shed wall. There will frequently be five or six females on the ground up to ten feet from the nesting holes. They are either being mated, or they are grooming and exercising their wings, preparing to fly.

It is also important not to have filled birdbaths or ponds in or near the nesting areas. We find drowned bees in standing bodies of water near the nesting areas. I presume they go to the water to drink. Each year my wife hangs a shallow platter-shaped birdbath from the garden house roof just feet from my nesting colony. I forget about its dangers until I find the first six or eight drowned bees. The birdbath is quickly banned until after the nesting season.

In our garden the searching female has no problem finding a suitable nesting hole. Beside the nesting blocks from which the bees are emerging are new, clean 5/16-inch diameter nesting holes equalling six times the number of holes from which the bees are emerging. You must provide about six times more new nesting holes each year as the bees are capable of increase in that proportion from one year to the next.

Soon the pregnant female and each of her sisters has found a hole to her liking and has marked it with her individual pheromone to provide a scent identity. She has staked her claim to that nest hole and no other bee will use it. It will be her home until she has filled it with nest cells. Then she will move on.

Having found her home, the female bee is off looking for mud, pollen and nectar with which to build and provision her first cell. The Orchard Mason does not range great distances in its search for provisions,

perhaps not more than several hundred feet. Our expectant female first finds a deposit of moist soil or clay and collects enough of it to build a basal plug in her chosen hole. She then finds a source of pollen and nectar nearby. Hopefully it is the blossoms of several of the fruit trees now in bloom on the Belgian Fence. She gathers a full load of pollen, drinks in nectar, and then flies back to the hole. She scrapes off the pollen, regurgitates the nectar over it and then mixes the sticky pile with the tiny horns on her head.

Frequently the bee will emerge from the hole with her face completely yellow with the sticky mixture. By mid afternoon she has a nice little pile of food stacked up. First the pollen, then the nectar, then more pollen. Back and forth she speeds to the blossoms loading up all she can carry. Again and again she returns to the blossoms until finally the mixture and the top coating are just right. It is not known how she knows the proper amount of food to collect but she collects a larger pile for the female eggs, a pile about the size of a new pencil eraser.

Now with maternal precision she turns around and backs down the hole to the waiting food provisions. She carefully positions herself over the sticky mass, and deposits a small white egg directly into the waiting pollen and nectar. As she lays the egg her wings vibrate rapidly making a high pitched

sound easily heard outside of the nesting hole by the human ear.

The egg, three-millimeters long, is shaped like a wiener sausage with a wiener-like curve. One end is embedded in the food mass so that the egg sticks out erect. It almost shimmers with a translucent sort of glow. The egg is held into the moist mass by the surface tension of the food material. The liquid consistency of the mix is critical to the egg staying in place. Too moist, or too dry and the egg falls out. The female bee must judge the perfect moisture content and then she must seal the cell from the atmosphere so that moisture content does not diminish through dehydration.

Now the bee speeds out of the hole to the mud quarry, for the egg must be protected and another nesting chamber prepared for her next egg. The female flies off to a place on the ground where the proper dirt or clay exists. Moisture is important because our mother-to-be must now become a mason. She must be able to build with the dirt that she seeks. Finding soil of the proper moisture content, she rolls up a ball of mud mortar and, grasping it in her mandibles, flies back to the hole and her exposed egg. She attaches her mortar to the wall of the hole and returns for more.

By the end of the day she has completed the cell. She has constructed a circular wall, which seals off the nesting chamber almost like a rigid diaphragm. The egg is safe for now. It is late in the afternoon and our hard working bee is getting cold. She crawls head first into the nesting hole and there she will stay for the night. In the morning, when the sun warms the air almost to flying temperature, she will back out of the hole, awkwardly turn around, and then back into the hole to sit at the entrance with just her head in the sun, warming up to start the day. Meanwhile, within her another egg is maturing.

And so it goes for the next thirty or so days. She will begin work when the temperature rises to about fifty-five degrees Fahrenheit; she will cease when the temperature falls below that or the sun goes down. She will lay about thirty-four eggs in her brief life. Then she will die, her life's work left behind in a series of holes that she had to find.

By the first week of June in my garden all of her contemporaries will also have died: there will not be an Orchard Mason Bee to be seen.

Elsewhere life goes on. Back in the nesting chambers spread through the forest or concentrated in hundreds of holes in the wooden blocks, or cardboard tubes in our garden, the eggs are hatching. Actually hatching is not the proper word. Bird eggs hatch, with a dramatic rending of their shell, to reveal a complete, if immature, chick. Bee eggs evolve with far less drama.

Three or four days after it is laid, the egg begins the first of a long chain of transformations. It splits to reveal the larva, looking pretty much like the original egg, except that now it lies flat on the food provision. The larva hardly moves. It slowly descends to lie on the food provision, its eating end attached to the food with small hook-like mouthparts.

The hungry larva eats and eats. Over a period of

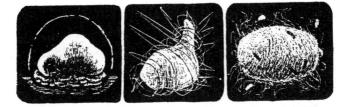

twenty-eight to twenty-nine days the food pile gets smaller and the larva gets larger. Finally the food is gone. During all but the last few days of this process the observer sees very little movement of the larva. It has simply been a great fat tubular lump ingesting all that rich food left behind by mama.

In the last few days it begins to defecate. Soon one can see small dark brown granule-like feces, which begin to collect at one end of the nesting chamber.

When the food has been entirely consumed there is a cessation of activity. Then, after several days of rest, the larva gets to work. Its anterior begins to revolve in a circular motion, frequently touching the sides of the cell wall as though sticking something up there. Around and around goes the rear end of the fat white larva, and finally after several hours the larva seems to disappear.

The observer begins to think his sight is failing as the larva slowly fades from view behind the thin veil it is spinning. It is slowly weaving a cocoon about itself with invisible thread.

When I first observed the weaving, I noticed the faint veil effect in the evening before retiring. When I awoke eight hours later, the larva had disappeared and in its place was an opaque, pinkish-white cocoon. A small miracle had taken place overnight.

The cocoon slowly turns color until in a few days

it is a rather dark, Chesapeake Retriever brown. It will have a few fecal granules woven into the outside layer, and it will be very tough. Its interior is varnished with a waterproof substance. It is surprisingly resistant to cutting, even with sharp scissors. Clearly the cocoon is an effective, strong, and, I presume, well insulated home for the long, cold winter ahead.

After what must have been a Herculean effort in spinning the cocoon, the larva enters a month-long period of inactivity, apparently resting from its labors. Then it changes into a pupa. In the pupal stage our bee-to-be begins to show some of its final shape. It rather looks like an insect mummy with many of the body parts now apparent but encased tightly in the pupal case.

Within the case great changes are occurring. After several weeks the final molt occurs and a complete imago, or adult bee, rests within the protective confines of the cocoon. It began in March or April — all through the summer the changes continued — and now it is September and the metamorphosis is complete.

The now-adult bee lies in its cocoon ready to go. However, Mother Nature in her wisdom is not ready for our little friend yet. In September there is nothing to pollinate. If it is nature's intent that the Orchard Mason be her pollinator the bee must sleep through the winter and emerge in the spring with the blossoms. And so it happens. Through the cold winter the bees lie in their insulated cocoons, further insulated by wood, protected from predators by the mud walls erected by their mothers. There they lie until spring when they awake to undertake their crucial role in the balance of nature: pollination.

The life history of the Orchard Mason is only one of natures' small miracles. Nevertheless its intricate balance and incredible practicality fill me with awe. If you share my fascination to this point perhaps you will also enjoy some of the small facts about this life story.

The female, when laying eggs, is able to determine the sex of the egg she is laying. When she was mated by one or more males, the semen she received was stored in a special organ in her body called a spermatheca. By applying some of that semen onto an egg as it passes through the egg-laying channel she creates a female. When she withholds semen from a passing egg she destines it to be a male. She intentionally lays female eggs first, in the back cells of a long nesting hole. Production of female progeny is most important for continuing the species, and they are thus best protected from predators. The hapless males occupying the front chambers are sacrificed to any invaders, hopefully satisfying them, or at least slowing them down until the females can escape in the spring. It only takes one male to impregnate many females. On average two-thirds of the eggs laid are males. They are effective sacrifices to divert the enemy at the gate.

More than ninety percent of the females emerge in a two-hour period in the morning, from 9:00 AM to

11:00 AM. At this time of day the ambient temperature is low and humidity levels are high. It is postulated that large quantities of the female attractant pheromone are released during this time, and that the dissipation rate of the attractant is reduced because of the lower temperature and higher humidity. Thus the odds are improved that the males will find the females and that the propagation of the species will be assured. Whatever the cause, the morning emergence and the resulting mating frenzy are obvious to the observer. The patrolling males increase their flying speed and aggressiveness noticeably. The buzzing sound of the flying bees seems to increase in pitch and intensity. One is reminded of the feeding frenzy of sharks or a flock of sea birds. Each newly emerged female is immediately grasped by a waiting male and frequently two, sometimes three, late arriving males land on the pile contesting for the coveted mating position.

The females gather wet soil to build the masonry walls of the nesting cells. The soil must be of just the right moisture content. To get the correct mixture the bees will excavate a "mine," digging down to the proper moisture content. In my garden I sometimes dig with a shovel a hole down through the soil until I reach clay. The resultant hole is about sixteen inches deep. Ten minutes after I have dug it, the bees have found it and dozens of them are trading back and forth between the "mine" and the nesting colony. How did they find it? How did they communicate its location?

In another instance this year a neighbor reported many mason bees "nesting" in a crevice between the rocks in a low wall in his front yard. A quick inspection revealed the truth. They were not nesting, they were mining. Somehow they had found nice clay behind those rocks. They were busily mining it and transporting it the two hundred and fifty feet across Knox Avenue, around our house and into the nesting holes in my bee colony. It was interesting to watch the heavily laden bees headed for home, flying just a foot or two above the neighbor's lawn, seemingly unable to quickly achieve altitude. I wondered if they were looking both ways before crossing the busy street.

Each cell partition takes eight to twelve mud-collecting trips. Provisioning each cell with the required pollen and nectar takes fourteen to thirty-five foraging trips.

When the female has filled her nesting hole with cells, each with its egg, she always leaves a gap between the outer wall of the last cell and the beginning of the thick entrance plug. Scientists call this gap the "vestibule." The making of a vestibule is a common practice among almost all hole-nesting solitary bees. Do they do this as a protective device? I surmise that the vestibule creates enough distance between the hole opening and the first cell wall to prevent most birds from reaching the bee in that first cell. Many times I have had birds, such as Downey woodpeckers, peck out the entrance plug but not get to a bee.

In the cell the female kneads the mud to an even consistency with her mandibles. She then applies the mud by pressing it with her revolving body, finishing and polishing the masonry with the horns on her head. She carefully seals the back of a nesting hole, filling in any cracks and uneven areas to provide a slightly concave wall for the back of the first cell.

The life history of the Orchard Mason Bee, fascinating as it is, is not unique in the world of solitary bees. The basic features of its way of life are repeated by thousands of other bee species. The gathering of pollen and nectar, the preparation of a nesting cell, an egg inserted into the food provision, the spinning of a cocoon, and finally the long winter rest and emergence in spring or summer, are the common denominators of solitary bee existence. This shared life history is what makes them such valuable pollinators for the Earth's plants.

The unique variations of this life story are what make the study of the solitary bees so interesting. Some bees dig nests into the ground, some burrow into wood, many must find a hole provided by others. One species nests only in the spiraled labyrinth of the abandoned shell of a particular species of snail.

Chapter 3

Pollination

If you believe nature has a purpose for all Earth's creatures, then you just have to believe that the Orchard Mason Bee was put on this Earth to pollinate.

Let's discuss for a minute the pollination of an ordinary backyard apple. If you remember your high school biology, you will know that the apple blossom has a number of stamens. These are the male components of the blossom. At the tip of the stamen is the pollen-bearing anther. Think of the pollen as the sperm of the flower world. In the center of the blossom are the styles, at the tips of which are the five stigmas. These are the female parts of the flower. Each style has a hollow passageway that leads down through the blossom to the ovaries.

Pollen from the anthers of one apple cultivar must somehow find its way to the stigmatic surfaces of

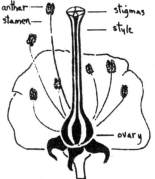

compatible but different apple cultivars during the short period of stigma receptivity. To make things more difficult, at least two pollen granules must enter each stigma for successful pollination. The pollen grows down the tube in the stigma to the ovary where fertilization takes place.

If several of the stigmas fail to receive the required pollen, their connected ovaries will not develop seeds and that apple will be lopsided and not marketable. If the pollen from a compatible apple fails to find its way to our blossom there will be no fruit at all, and finally, the temperature must be at least fifty-five degrees Fahrenheit before germination can occur. The next time you eat a delicious apple fresh from the tree, pause a moment and consider the natural wonders that created it. But wait! — There is more to ponder.

The essential transfer of pollen from blossom to blossom occurs in many ways. Wind and air currents accomplish some of it. Insects of many kinds contribute to the job. Flies, butterflies, and moths, including the nocturnal species, all help. For some night-blooming desert plants, nectar-eating bats are the chief pollinators.

The best of the pollinators, however, are the bees. They accomplish perhaps eighty-five percent of the world's pollination. Bees trade only in pollen and nectar. It is one of the characteristics that distinguishes them from their *Hymenopteran* cousins, the wasps. Adult bees feed only on nectar, the fuel that powers their remarkable activity. They gather pollen only to feed to their young, for it is the pollen that carries the all-important proteins that build bee body structure. Many wasps are also powered by nectar, but they must feed their carnivorous larvae only meat. Thus wasps are hunters while bees are gatherers.

Because all bees gather pollen and nectar, all bees are pollinators. Therefore all bees are beneficial creatures. Watch your flowers and shrub blossoms closely this spring and summer. You will be amazed at the diversity of bees that visit doing their accidental work of pollination while gathering the pollen and nectar essential to carrying on their species.

The great commercial pollinators of the world are the widely used European honeybees (Apis mellifera). They exist in incredible numbers, are highly transportable and have social habits that man has adapted to his use for thousands of years. Perhaps the best proof of their symbiotic relationship with man is the fact that the English colonists brought honeybees with them to North America. They were imported to the Jamestown, Virginia colony sometime before 1638. North America does not have a native honeybee.

Prior to the arrival of the European honeybee, the native fruits and flowers of North America were obviously being successfully pollinated. The best of the native pollinators were the estimated 3,500 species of wild bees that still inhabit North America. The vast majority of those bees are solitary bees much like our Orchard Mason.

The importance of our native bee species was long

ignored because of the successful qualities of the European honeybees, but they are being ignored no longer. The honeybee in North America and much of the rest of the world is under siege by two predatory mites that have swept the globe. These mites, accidently imported to North America by the honeybee queen industry, have destroyed ninety percent of the feral honeybees of this continent and have placed severe stress on the populations of honeybees raised and tended by man for agricultural purposes. Commercial beekeepers are able to keep their colonies alive only by careful and expensive miticide applications to their hives. Agriculture teeters on the brink of a pollination crisis.

Entomologists and many people in agriculture are now looking carefully at the pollination alternatives offered by native bees. Pollination by native bees has always played a massive and important role in the life cycles of not only native plants but of some of our commercial agricultural crops as well. Many of these wild bees are much better pollinators of specific plants than the honeybee.

Studies by USDA/ARS researchers at Utah State University have established that the Orchard Mason, bee for bee, is far more efficient as a pollinator of apples, pears, cherries, and almonds than the honeybee. "How can that be?" you might ask. The answer lies in both bee biology and differences in life style.

Remember watching the honeybee in your garden? She flies from blossom to blossom carefully plucking pollen granules, wetting them with a bit of nectar and stuffing them into the tiny "pollen baskets" on her legs. This efficient and tidy method of

carrying pollen does not aid in pollination. It is too neat and clean. The wetted pollen does not fall from her "pollen baskets" as she lands on the next blossom, thus it cannot pollinate. Most of her pollination is done by pollen granules that have accidently caught on her body hairs.

Our Orchard Mason is not as sophisticated as the honeybee. She has no leg pockets at all. She must carry pollen by wedging the granules into rows of stiff specialized hairs that cover her abdomen. This pollen-carrying adaptation is called the scopa. Her scopa does a good job of carrying pollen, but some falls out as the bee tries to stuff more and more into this primitive cargo rack. It is kind of like stuffing rice grains into a hairbrush. It carries plenty but spills a lot also. She is dragging her scopa over every blossom she visits, and she visits plenty.

The Orchard Mason holds another advantage in the pollination derby. Her entire body is much hairier than the honeybee. Consequently she carries around more pollen caught in her body hair. As she crawls over the blossoms she redistributes much of the pollen, some of it to the stigma of a compatible fruit.

Greg Dickman, in his brochure, *Orchard Bees*, states that the Orchard Mason visits more blossoms each day than the honey bee, and pollinates a much higher percentage of those blooms visited. He states that the honeybee visits an average seven hundred blooms daily. It pollinates only thirty of them, a mere five percent success rate. He further claims that our Orchard Mason pollinates 1600 flowers per day, a success rate of ninety-five to ninety-nine percent. Philip Torchio, at USDA/ARS, Utah State, questions the validity of Dickman's numbers suggesting that the definitive study has not been done.

It remains clear, however, that the Orchard Mason is a far better pollinator of early fruits and nuts, than the honeybee. This advantage results from a number of biological and behavioral features of both the bee and the blossom.

In many cultivars of apples, the blossom is so shaped that the honeybee, foraging for nectar, lands on the blossom petal and never touches the anther which bears the pollen. The Orchard Mason of both sexes always lands on the sexual column of any apple flower.

The Orchard Mason flits nervously from tree to tree as it forages. In contrast, the honeybee will spend a lot of time on one tree, going from blossom to blossom in a small area on that tree. As most apples require cross-pollination, the Orchard Mason's nervous habits make it far more likely to transfer pollen from one tree species to another. The essential cross-pollination is achieved because the Orchard Mason has visited many trees while the honeybee diligently filled her pollen bags from but one tree.

A further advantage stems from the fact that the Orchard Mason initiates daily flight at a temperature of thirteen degrees centigrade, or fifty-five degrees Fahrenheit — just the temperature at which apple pollen will germinate. The honeybee, guided by its southern European genes, begins flight at a little warmer temperature and so misses some time at work on early spring mornings. Conversely, any insect operating at temperatures colder than the germination temperature of apple pollen will not be effective as a pollinator.

The Orchard Mason Bee fits the apple very nicely. Studies demonstrate that maximum pollination in a commercial apple orchard can be achieved with as few as two hundred and fifty female Orchard Masons per acre. Compare that with the standard orchardist's practice of providing one honeybee hive for each two acres of orchard. A honeybee hive is apt to contain forty thousand bees, a large percentage of which are foragers.

Faced with the evidence of the Orchard Mason's superiority as a pollinator, one is quick to ask, "Why aren't there more of them and why are they not used commercially?" The essential part of the answer is found in the experienced conservatism of the agricultural world. Generations of orchardists have been raised with the sure knowledge that honeybees will pollinate our nation's fruits and nuts. Furthermore, a substantial industry has developed over the years that transports honeybees to the blossoms. Traveling from south to north each spring, the beekeepers rent their bees and their pollination services by the acre. The rental fees are reasonable, the bees do their job each year as they have for generations. Why would the orchardist want to change?

In my opinion, the honeybee will not face serious competition in the agricultural fields and orchards of America until one of two things happen.

Further decline in the domestic honeybee population caused by the scourge of the tracheal and varroa mites would throw agriculture into a pollination crisis, demanding alternative pollinators. Or, secondly, an enterprising person arrives on the scene who will contract to provide Orchard Mason Bee pollination services. Those services could include delivering bees to the orchard each spring, the provision and tending of nesting habitat, moving bees from orchard to orchard, and consulting with the farmer on appropriate plantings of pollen and nectar bearing plants to supplement the food supplies of the agricultural crop.

Dr. Torchio has been studying commercial applications of the bee for many years. It now appears that, when done properly, the bees can be moved successfully from orchard to orchard. I rather suspect that the Orchard Mason Bee will fulfill its destiny as a commercial pollinator only when farmers or farm corporations commit to propagating the bees on site to pollinate their own crops.

In the meantime, I will continue to encourage the use of the Orchard Mason for the home gardener and for the urban dweller to which honeybees have become an endangered and seldom seen species.

Several species of solitary bees have already established themselves as successful pollinators of major agricultural crops. For many years the alkali bee, *Nomia melanderi,* was a major pollinator of seed alfalfa in the irrigated desert country of eastern Washington, Oregon, and Idaho. The other undoubted commercial success is the Alfalfa Leafcutter bee, *Megachile rotundata.*

These two solitary bees have become the continent's pollinators of seed alfalfa because the honeybee turned down the job. Honeybees simply don't like alfalfa. The bee, probing into the alfalfa blossom, triggers a snapping mechanism, which thumps the bee on the head as the price for receiving its stores of pollen and nectar. Honeybees apparently are not pugilists. Mostly, they refuse to fight.

By accident and observation it was discovered that an immigrant from East Asia, *Megachile rotundata,* a tiny leafcutter bee, was not bothered by repeated blows to the head. It was easy to propagate, did the job well, and soon an industry developed selling the bees, nesting habitat, and pollination services to the seed alfalfa growers.

In Japan, a native solitary bee, *Osmia cornifrons,* the "horn-faced bee," has for thirty-five years been the principal pollinator of Japan's apple crop. The bees are wintered in the fruit cold storage warehouses. They are held there until just before the bloom and then released to do their work. Year after year, generation after generation, the horn-faced bee does its job.

Osmia cornifrons was imported to the United States in the early 1990s largely due to the efforts of a USDA entomologist, Suzanne Batra. Her passion for the attributes of this pretty little bee has resulted in its introduction to many parts of the country. Its life history is essentially identical to that of the Orchard Mason and many backyard gardeners have a mixed population, *Osmia lignaria* and *Osmia cornifrons* nesting together in the same nesting blocks. There is some evidence that *O. cornifrons* is not as winter hardy as the Orchard Mason, but I have a number of acquaintances that use them very successfully.

Pollination of the world around us is one of nature's great processes, Year after year the floral world renews itself with this intricate, complicated, and largely unnoticed sexual process. With the possible exception of those poor souls that suffer from hay fever, man takes the blessings of pollination for granted. We would do well to understand its importance as well as the delicate balance that its success rests upon.

Perhaps the following story will illustrate the fragility of successful pollination.

For years I had heard that honeybees did not favor pear blossoms, and that, consequently pears were difficult to pollinate. One day, during a visit to Dr. Torchio at his home in Utah, I asked him if this was true.

His answer fascinates me to this day. He told me that pear nectar is not very viscous, that in fact it is quite thick and syrupy. So much so that it is difficult for the bees to suck it into their honey stomachs. As a result the bees will pass up the thick pear nectar if they have a better choice. Torchio went on to say that "orchardists have learned to expect better pear crops after a wet winter." The reason; the pear trees draw up more water during the wet season and the pear nectar becomes diluted and more viscous. Pear nectar is easier for the bees to collect in those years and so they temporarily shelve their disdain for pear blossoms.

Adequate pollination of North America and indeed the entire world is an issue linked to the very survival of man on this planet. Edward O. Wilson, writing in the Foreword, of Buchmann and Nabhan's important book, *The Forgotten Pollinators*, states that "Eighty percent of the species of our food plants worldwide, we are informed, depend on pollination by animals, almost all of which are insects. One of every three mouthfuls of food we eat, and of the beverages we drink, are delivered to us roundabout by a volent bestiary of pollinators."

Learning to identify, protect and use our native bees is an activity worthy of each of our best efforts.

Chapter 4

Similar Species

The Orchard Mason Bee is not the only solitary bee pollinating our world. In fact there may be thirty thousand species of solitary bees on the planet. They represent ninety-nine percent of all bee species and are more numerous than all the Earth's birds and mammals combined.

Their diversity is incredible. The smallest are no more than two millimeters in length, the size of an aphid. The largest approach eighty millimeters, about three inches. Some nest only in existing holes, while others drill their own nesting tunnels in wood or earth. Some are nocturnal, others fly only at dawn or dusk. Many bees, like the Orchard Mason, have a wide distribution over huge areas. Some bee species are specific to a particular township. They all share one important trait. None of them make honey.

These non-honeybees have complicated biologies. In most the adult form is short-lived and their nesting sites are often difficult to locate. Some produce offspring only every other year, and they are usually small in population and very easy to overlook.

In terms of biomass, the total weight of all the individuals of one species on the Earth, the honeybees probably surpass all of the solitary bees put together (or did before the mite infestation). The highly successful social insects such as honeybees, ants, and termites, together comprise a huge percentage of insect biomass, and for that matter, the Earth's biomass.

Edward O. Wilson, a world authority on ants, says in an essay for the Xerces Society magazine, *Wings*, "The ants and termites, the most highly social of all organisms, plus the social wasps and social bees which rival them in colonial organization, make up about eighty percent of the biomass."

That incredible statement is a clear illustration of the advantages of social organization. The Earth's biomass includes the combined body weight of every man, animal, reptile, fish, and insect. Just think of it: everything on Earth that walks, crawls, swims, flies or slithers. Eighty percent of that combined weight is attributed to the social insects.

The social insects comprise a tiny percentage of the number of species, but a huge percentage of the number of individuals. Who says it doesn't pay to be organized.

The Orchard Mason Bee has competitors vying for its nesting sites and food supply. Depending upon where you live, your Orchard Masons may be coexisting with some of the bees described in this chapter. You may wish to identify and propagate some of these alternative bees to fit your own interests and goals. You will recall that we have discussed the two subspecies of *Osmia lignaria, Osmia lignaria propinqua Cresson* and its eastern cousin, *Osmia lignaria lignaria* Say.

Now let's meet—

Osmia californica Cresson

Osmia californica Cresson is a leaf cutter bee that emerges about the time the Orchard Mason is at its peak of activity. This bee competes with the Orchard Mason for nesting holes where their ranges overlap.

It is mainly a pollinator of plants in the family *Compositae*. This bee has a similar lifestyle except that it does not use mud to construct its nesting cells. It uses a composite pulp made of macerated leaf and soil. Pieces are cut from the leaves of specific plants and chewed into a pulp ball which is then rolled in soil until coated. The leaf/soil  ball is then carried to the nest hole where it is further processed by chewing until it becomes the desired consistency to make the cell division walls. The composite mixture is strengthened with a coating of nectar that hardens as it dries.

The offspring of *Osmia californica* may spend either one or two winters in the nesting cell. One generation of the bee can emerge over a two-year period, some maturing this year and some next. This seemingly random maturation process is called parsivoltinism.

Osmia montana montana Cresson

This bee also competes with the Orchard Mason for nesting holes where they share the same range. Another leafcutter, this bee emerges one to two weeks after *O. californica.* It constructs its nesting cells with pure leaf pulp, which is not mixed with soil. This bee is also parsivoltine. Sometimes overwintering larvae and overwintering adults are found in adjacent cells in the same nesting hole. If larvae, destined to spend two winters in the cell, happen to be in the forward cells, their adult brothers or sisters will destroy them as they struggle to emerge in an earlier spring.

Nomia melanderi (Alkali Bee)

A bee of the western deserts, this bee is an effective pollinator of alfalfa when the crop is bordered by alkali flats where the bee nests. The alkali bee is about 2/3 the size of the honeybee and is identified by gold to turquoise abdominal stripes. It nests in large populations in the soil of alkali flats. Each nest has a main burrow leading from the entrance hole to a carved-out chamber, twelve to sixty centimeters below the soil surface. A cluster of six to twenty-two elongate cells is constructed below the chamber and each is oriented vertically. Each cell is coated with a waterproofing secretion, which protects the cell's occupant even during periodic flooding of the flats.

The alkali bee provisions its cells with nectar and pollen and lays a single egg in each. The cell is then

capped with a soil plug. The
larva overwinters, pupates
in the spring, and the adult
alkali bee digs out of the soil
in May or June to repeat the
cycle.

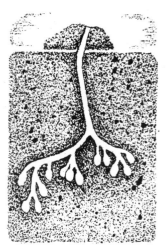

The alkali bee visits a
wide variety of flowering
plants including alfalfa, clover, onion and mint crops.
It has been a valuable pollinator of commercial crops
for many years. Its nesting
sites have been successfully replicated and managed
so that this bee remains a valuable agricultural pollinator in its range.

Megachile rotundata (Alfalfa Leafcutting Bee)

This is a Eurasian bee that was accidentally introduced on the East Coast of North America in the
early 1930s. Like many hole nesters it probably ar-
rived in a load of wood from another continent. It
apparently first became established near Washington D.C. and rapidly migrated across the continent
where it reached the Pacific Northwest sometime prior
to the 1950s.

Soon afterwards, alfalfa seed growers in Utah and
Idaho began noticing the bee visiting the bloom in
their fields. Subsequent studies of this newcomer
established its unique value in alfalfa pollination and
determined a viable way to commercially propagate
this bee. The entire West is now the beneficiary of
this successful creature and it has been reintroduced

to Europe and other parts of the world as the dominant pollinator of alfalfa, an important feed resource for cattle.

This bee is about half the size of the honeybee. Its abdomen is striped with bands of light colored hair. It carries pollen in its scopa as does *Osmia lignaria.* It nests in existing holes and constructs its cell partitions by overlapping circular sections of leaf that it cuts. The pieces are purposely overlapped, the edges chewed and tamped into place. The chewed areas of leaf dry and form strong bonding lines interconnecting the overlapped leaf pieces. The result is a bullet-shaped leaf cell.

Pollen and nectar are gathered, deposited in the cell and a single egg is laid in the deposit. The female then seals the cell with circular leaf pieces chewed and tamped into place. She then begins another cell immediately on top of the first.

Modern propagation of this valuable bee involves large nesting boards or shelters, with drilled holes set in the alfalfa fields. A drive through western alfalfa country will reveal these boards, looking for all the world like signboards standing in the flat fields.

Osmia cornifrons (Horned-Faced Bee)

This small orange striped bee is a native of Japan. At one time it was being distributed in the United States by the U.S. Department of Agriculture, which had concluded that the bee had valuable commercial potential.

O. cornifrons has long been used for fruit pollination in Japan where it is cultivated extensively. It has shown some difficulty in surviving severe winters in North America, but has been successfully established in a number of areas.

It competes with Orchard Masons for nesting sites. Because it is about two-thirds the size of the Orchard Mason it can utilize smaller nesting holes, but is quite happy with a 5/16-inch hole favored by the Orchard Mason. The author knows of a bee fancier in the Pacific Northwest who introduced *O. cornifrons* into his urban lot. They share his Orchard Mason nesting blocks and he can no longer keep them separate. They coexist nicely.

Osmia coerulescens

This bee is a species native to Europe. It is abundant throughout France and Spain and was introduced accidentally into the United States. It is apparently an effective pollinator of red clover but has not been developed commercially. Shortly after writing the first edition of *The Orchard Mason Bee*, I had the opportunity to spend several springs in Europe. I searched at every opportunity for *Osmia coerulescens* without success. Imagine my surprise when upon returning home, I found a strange dark bee visiting nesting blocks that I had installed several blocks from my home. I sent specimens off to be identified and they were declared to be *Osmia coerulescens*. This hardy little traveler had migrated all the way across the continent to the shores of the Pacific in Northwest Washington State. I now have a small colony working each summer in my garden. They normally emerge in mid-June and are active for several months.

Osmia sanrafaelae

This species is restricted to the San Rafael Desert in Southern Utah. It's an effective pollinator of alfalfa, and will nest in man-made nesting materials.

Osmia rufa (Red Mason Bee)

This is the pre-eminent mason bee of Western Europe and the British Isles. Its life history is virtually identical to that of North America's Orchard Mason Bee and it can be successfully propagated by the European gardener using the same methods described herein for the Orchard Mason. If there is any difference in nesting habits it might be that *O. rufa* shows a decided interest in cracks and crevices in stone work in addition to its willingness to nest in holes in wood and other materials.

I captured the *Osmia rufa* that I have in my collection while negotiating a canal lock in France on a warm spring day in 1997. I had just steered our barge into the ancient stone lock. The gates had closed behind us and the lock-keeper opened the gate valve to let in the water which would raise us to the canal ahead. As I stood in the pilothouse, monitoring our slow progress up the lock wall, I suddenly saw a little rufous colored bee investigating cracks in the mortar between the old cut stone. I quickly grabbed an empty wineglass and a piece of stiff paper that were, fortunately, nearby and captured the bee. By the time the lock had filled I had my specimen secured for my collection.

On a visit to France and Great Britain in 1999, I learned that the honeybees of Europe have suffered the same fate at the hands of the tracheal and varroa mites, as have their counterparts in North America. *Osmia rufa* should be able to play the same spring pollinator role in Europe that *Osmia lignaria* does for North America. I expect to see an awakening of interest in its propagation among the many passionate gardeners on that side of the Atlantic.

Heriades carinata (Onion Bee)

This tiny bee is a great surprise and a bonus to my summer garden. I am sure it has been an occupant of my vegetable garden for all the years that I have grown one, but I had never noticed it until last summer. As I write this a large and thriving colony of them is nesting in wooden blocks on a sunny post beside the corn patch.

They are gathering pollen and nectar from a variety of flowers, but are especially abundant on the great purple balls which are the blossoms of the leeks. I am calling it the "Onion Bee" because it is clear to me that the onion represents one floral family that this bee will pollinate. I don't yet fully understand what other plants they will pollinate. In addition to the leeks, I see them on roses, marjoram, oregano, and goldenrod. It appears that they are generalists as feeders, which could make them valuable mid-summer vegetable pollinators.

I can attest to the delight I am experiencing as I watch them bringing their pollen and nectar back to the tiny 1/8-inch holes in the fir nesting blocks that I have provided.

I learned about the bee by putting out a small observation nesting block with different sized holes. The smallest holes were only 1/8-inch. First I was excited to discover the *Passaloecus* wasp described in Chapter 6. Two weeks later I was astonished to find a horde of these tiny *Megachilid* bees nesting in the same nesting block.

This bee is only about 5/16-inch long. It is black, with light colored bands on its abdomen. It carries its pollen, like the Orchard Mason, in a scopa underneath its abdomen. It is distinctly a warm weather bee, choosing to stay in its warm nesting hole until the thermometer rises to sixty-five degrees Fahrenheit.

This bee is very easy to propagate. The 1/8-inch holes in our "Aphid Eater" nesting blocks are just the right size for the bee. I am making arrangements now to propagate many of these pleasant and interesting little pollinators and will have them available for sale beginning the winter of 1999.

As you can see, the Orchard Mason Bee is not the only choice for the backyard fruit grower who wishes to improve pollination. It does appear to this writer, however, that the Orchard Mason might be the best choice. It apparently is tolerant of a wider range of climactic conditions, and because it favors fruit blossoms but will utilize many other flowers and even dandelions, it will prosper where more specialized bees would not.

The geographic range of the Orchard Mason is so widespread and general that it is entirely possible that you, the reader, have the Orchard Mason in your yard already. If so, the following chapter on propagation will contain all that you need to know to establish your own population of these efficient pollinators.

Chapter 5

Propagation

You have read about the fascinating life history of the Orchard Mason Bee. Now all you need do to develop a healthy population of bees to pollinate your own fruits and flowers is use that knowledge in a practical way.

First you must locate a native population of bees or purchase a starting colony. Remember that our friend is native to every state west of the Rockies, and its close cousin lives in most of the states east of the Rockies. If you are very lucky, you may have them in your backyard right now. You may never have seen them, but then, you didn't know what to look for previously, did you? Look for the bees on the earliest spring blossoms. Look in your own yard. Take long walks perusing the neighborhood shrubs, and be sure to wander in your city parks, rural woodlands, or wherever you see new blossoms, for there you will find the Orchard Mason.

Once you have located the bees, or received your purchased bees in the mail, you must provide nesting holes for them. You can expect a nice increase each year. I strongly recommend using the new "System" nesting tubes because of their many advantages but you may wish to start out by simply drilling holes in scraps of wood. If you choose the latter all you need do is drill 5/16-inch holes in a block of wood to create a nesting trap described later in this chapter.

Your nesting habitat should be hung at the populated site at the end of February or whenever the weather begins to warm. By the first of June, you should have a trap full of bee eggs that you can carefully bring home.

You might set up a trapline. Make or purchase a number of nesting devices and set them out in more than one place. Try the walls of a shingled building, or warm sheltered spots in your friends' gardens. Don't bother to hang them on fence posts or in trees; those are the bee's least favorite places. Concentrate on warm sunny walls of buildings under an eave where they will get rain protection but far enough below the eave so that they are still in the sunshine. If you hang your traps on a succession of friends' garages around town you are apt to find the bees somewhere. Your only risk is that your friends might think you a little strange.

If you are not lucky enough to find bees your first spring, or if you wish to be sure to get a colony started, you may want to buy bees. See the last page of this book for particulars.

Let's assume that you have a few bees using your yard. The challenge then is to create an environment in which they can prosper and multiply. Like any of God's creatures, our winged friends need ample food,

"Nesters" mounted in Knox Cellars' Cedar Shelter.

shelter in which to nest, and finally, an environment, which at the very least does not kill them.

The food that sustains the Orchard Mason Bee is of course, pollen and nectar from the flowers of trees and plants. The Orchard Mason, unlike some of the wild bees, is not a very fussy feeder. It will use the blossoms of a wide range of plants for its sustenance. I have observed the bees on dandelions, scrubs and flowers of all kinds, and most importantly, on fruit trees.

It is vital that your location has not only a good supply of blossoms, but also a supply of blossoms over the entire period that the bees are foraging. In the Pacific Northwest that period is roughly from March 15th to June 1st. Of course, the bees' emergence depends on the weather. Your local emergence time might be many weeks later than mine, but you can count on nature to time their emergence with the appearance of the first blossoms. From year to year that blossom/emergence date might vary by as much as a month, so try to be patient.

Optimum bee propagation requires that you have more than just fruit blossoms to feed your bees. The

fruit tree blossom period is short. Most fruit varieties bloom and wither in little more than a week. If
you had but one variety of fruit in your yard, and no
other blooms of any kind, your poor bees would eat
and lay eggs for only the week that your fruit blossomed.

After your blooms were finished, the bees would
have no choice but to leave your yard for a location
with a food supply of longer duration. The eggs they
had laid in your nests would be perfectly good. It is
just that you would be getting but seven or eight
nesting cells from each female that you released. Your

carefully nurtured females
would be laying another
twenty five eggs or so in
someone else's garden. In order to increase your bee
population and keep them
for the long term, you must
plant for variety and sustained pollen yield.

I heartily recommend that
you plant the *Pieris japonica*
shrub if it will thrive in your
climate. This large evergreen
shrub does very well in the wet parts of the Pacific
Northwest where I live, although I have been told
that it is not winter hardy in the extreme cold states
of the mid-west and east coast. Your local nursery
should be able to advise you. The *Sunset Garden Book*
shows it as *Pieris japonica (Andromeda japonica)*. Its
chief feature is cascades of tiny bell-like blossoms
that bloom very early in the spring and continue for
weeks and weeks. In the very cool spring of 1999 it

was still blooming and feeding bees on the 20th of May.

My bees seem to love it and feed on it all through the blossom time. Our *Pieris japonica* stands ten feet from the bee colony, large and accessible. I think it may be an important factor in the six hundred percent increase in bee population I enjoy most years.

Further evidence of the *Pieris japonica's* attraction for the Orchard Mason is given by the remarkable number of Orchard Masons that visit a group of the shrubs planted in the landscaping of a downtown bank in my city. The bank is situated in the center of a typical asphalt and concrete downtown environment, but somewhere nearby, there is a thriving Orchard Mason colony. Each spring I am astonished by the feeding frenzy that I see on those shrubs. When loaded with pollen, our little black friends dash off across the busy city street to the west of the bank and disappear. I have tried to follow them to their homes without success. Perhaps next year I will find the nesting site. It ought to be a great location to hang a few of my nesting blocks. I would like some of that city-tough strain in my breeding stock.

Osmia lignaria does not range far in its quest for food, perhaps no further than the length of a football field in any direction. A dense urban location becomes a great advantage when this fact is considered. My bee colony is in the old section of a small city. The building lots were platted with twenty-five foot widths. While most of the houses are built on two or even three lots, the neighborhood density is very high. It is also an area of very serious gardeners. There are a variety of trees, shrubs and flowers within the bees' range and consequently, my bees don't want for sources of food during their short lifetimes.

The bees must not only find pollen and nectar to feed themselves; they must find and transport the food provision for up to thirty-five nesting cells. There is a direct relationship between the abundance of food sources and the number of cells prepared and eggs laid in the life of a female. There is, further, a relationship between the food supply and the size of the offspring.

One would suppose that the larger the offspring, the better they are able to cope with the trials of life and the more successful they will be in reproducing themselves.

Other factors being equal, the single most important element in developing a large Orchard Mason Bee population is housing. The bee must have a hole of a proper size available before it can reproduce. If you wish a large number of bees you must provide a large number of holes. It is just that simple. Remember that the Orchard Mason does not make its own nesting hole. It must find a hole, and some other creature must make the hole.

You can achieve remarkable increases in your backyard bee population simply by providing more and more nesting holes as your population grows. If you cease providing fresh holes year after year, your population must stay stable. It is even likely that it will decrease as the frustrated females will look elsewhere for clean holes to lay eggs in.

Let's begin with the size of the hole. We suggest that you use only a 5/16-inch or seven-millimeter hole. The bee will successfully nest in both smaller and larger holes, but it will not be as successful in a size other than 5/16 inch. It is also important to know that the depth of the hole has a bearing on your success with this bee. The bees will nest in any depth hole that they can build a cell in. Over many years I have had fine success with holes the length of a normal drill bit, 3-1/2 inches. However, now we know that you will reach the optimum female to male sex ratio using a six-inch hole. Holes shorter than six inches result in a higher percentage of males than the optimum 1/3 female to 2/3 male ratio. Since females do most of the pollination the six-inch hole should be your choice.

I don't know the maximum depth the bees would fill; however, as an experiment I set out 12-inch tubes one year and the bees filled them up.

I did not always believe that 5/16 inch was the proper size. Early in my experience with the Orchard Mason, I ran another experiment. I drilled a large nesting block with four different sized holes: twenty holes each of 1/4-inch, 5/16-inch, 3/8-inch, and, finally, huge looking 7/16-inch holes.

I hung the block in my nesting colony and was astonished to note that the bees filled every one of the 1/4-inch holes before they started on the larger holes. Their second choice was the 5/16, and finally the 3/8 inch. They never did use the 7/16-inch size.

I was elated. I had made a discovery and I felt very scientific and wise. All of my nesting blocks that year were drilled with 1/4-inch holes. They filled rapidly and I had the usual good percentage of increase in filled holes. I was quite self-satisfied. Several gardening writers were recommending 5/16-inch holes.

Washington State University had given the larger hole the nod.

I had proved them wrong. Clearly, I reasoned, the bees would choose the smallest hole they could fit into simply because they would have to haul less mud to seal the nesting cells. Everyone knows that Mother Nature is efficient above all else. How could all those experts have been so wrong?

It was mid-winter when I got my comeuppance. Dr. Torchio, at Utah State, sent me a paper that established that the Orchard Mason Bee lays a higher percentage of female eggs in the 5/16-inch hole than she does in the smaller 1/4-inch hole. So 5/16-inch wide and 6-inches deep is the ideal.

I was doing fine using the smaller holes, but I would have been doing better with the 5/16 inch. The rate of population increase will be improved using the larger holes. Ah, humility. What seems so obvious and logical to us mere mortals is not always so in natures' great scheme. I can find no logic to support the bee's choice of the larger hole so have simply rationalized it by reminding myself of another advantage of the larger hole. The 5/16-inch hole is far less likely to be plugged by swelling wood fibers and for that reason also it is a better size.

A hole drilled into a soft block of wood tends to contain uncut and torn wood fibers. When that block of wood is exposed to the weather, it will pick up moisture. The wood fiber ends that were laid back by the whirling drill bit will swell and straighten and tend to plug a small hole. This swelling problem can be reduced by using a very sharp drill bit that cuts the fibers cleanly. My experience says that a "brad point" drill bit is far superior to the standard "job-bers bit" which was really designed for cutting metal.

Not long ago Dr. Torchio came up with a new nest-ing system using a 6-inch heavy cardboard guard tube, a thin paper inner liner and a plaster of Paris plug to hold the tubes together and stop the end of the nesting hole. That tube system, somewhat modi-fied, has become the recognized method to both trap and trade in the bees.

Let's take a look at a variety of ways to provide nesting sites for the Orchard Mason that we are try-ing to attract and propagate. I shall discuss several of the common techniques, but remember that bee propagation is not rocket science. The bee, first and foremost, requires a hole. You are free to use your imagination as to the presentation of holes to the bee.

Wooden Blocks

This is the traditional nesting technique. I make my nesting blocks of an excellent grade of tight grained fir purchased from a local lumber proces-sor. Pine, fir or hemlock work equally well. Just be sure to use untreated wood. Any kind of scrap wood will work just fine. I know many people who visit a building site at the framing stage. They pick up the small scraps piled beside the cut-off saw. Two by fours, two by sixes work fine if drilled into the edge

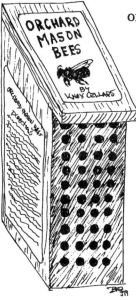

or the end so as to get the deepest possible holes.

In a four-inch deep block I drill a 5/16-inch hole to within 1/2 inch of the back. I don't think there is any reason you could not drill a hole twice that deep if you had wood thick enough and a drill bit long enough. Three and one half inches works, however. Be sure you don't drill all the way through the block. Predators can get in the back door that way and the bees will refuse to nest in them. Actually some people intentionally drill entirely through the block and then screw a wooden board to the back. They can then remove the board for the annual cleaning of the holes after the bees have emerged and are nesting in a clean block.

Drill the holes on 3/4-inch centers. In other words, the center of each hole should be 3/4 inch away from the center of all holes around it. I line all of my holes up in nice straight and square lines. I doubt that the bees care. I am sure that random holes drilled all over a piece of wood would suit them just as well. I simply prefer the look of a neatly laid out block. It also helps in counting completed holes as spring progresses, something that you will surely be doing.

Wooden blocks do have a problem with splitting. It is therefore important to select wood of as good quality as possible, and to use dry wood. I have never painted or treated my blocks; however I have read of others doing so before drilling them. If you must paint, you are well advised to do so well before the nesting season so that the drying paint volatiles will not drive the bees away. Acrylic paints should be used rather than oil based to limit the impact of the paint chemicals.

Here's a tip on drilling holes close to the edges of the blocks without splitting them. Simply clamp boards tightly on either side of the block. The inward pressure of the clamping technique will prevent split out as you drill.

I cut one end of the block at an angle tilting to the front and tack on a little piece of cedar shingle to shed rain. Then I drill one more hole at the top center of the backside of the block. This is the hanging hole. A nail driven into the outside wall of your house or out-building is now all you need to begin trapping the not-so-wily Orchard Mason Bee.

The wooden blocks can be used year after year, but you must be sure to clean out the holes each year. Failure to do so will result in a build-up of fungal and bacteria problems resulting from the large amounts of moisture in the nectar used in the food provision. That sweetened moisture soaks into the wood and creates a rich environment for the growth of health problems for your colony. In addition, mites and other predatory creatures linger in the old nesting holes, waiting to reinfest a new generation of bees.

It is my observation that persons who leave old nesting holes in their colony without doing something about hygiene begin to notice lots of unopened holes in the third spring. If you force bees to re-nest in the old holes and fail to provide new clean holes or clean out the old, your colony will fail to thrive and may eventually die out.

The bees will re-use the old uncleaned holes and seem to pull out the worst of the detritus from any hole they decide to use, but they will only use an old hole when there is no other choice. Year after year I watch the bees emerge and go directly to the new nesting holes that I provide. They will fill all of the new holes before any of them return to the old holes.

It is now my practice to remove all old nesting materials once I am convinced that the last of the females is out. I put the old wooden blocks in the firewood pile to warm me later in front of the winter fireplace. I replace each emptied seventy-eight hole nesting block with five or six new empty ones, or with the "System Nesters" and their seventy-four tubes, each six inches long. When the bees have almost filled those new nesting holes I add more nesting devices, little by little, until the season ends.

At about this time I do a night-time count of the nesting females. By shining a flashlight into the still unfinished holes I am able to accurately count how many females are still nesting. I want a new empty hole for each bee that I see. If my count reveals two hundred females I will mount three more "Nesters," a total of two hundred twenty-two holes. When those are beginning to fill, I will do a recount and put out some more nesting holes. I want the bees to fill each nesting trap, be it wooden block or system "Nester," so I dole them out late in the season, just one at a time.

After the emergence I throw away the old wood blocks and the soiled paper liners in order to destroy what disease and parasites might lurk in them. I am sure that my nesting populations are healthier and more mite free since I have adopted this practice. If you wish to save your old nesting blocks you will need to rotate them each year. Here is how you can do that.

Early in the spring before the bees emerge set new or at least clean nesting blocks beside the occupied blocks. When the bees emerge, almost all of them will begin nesting in the clean blocks, ignoring the holes that they just emerged from. When you are convinced that all of the females have emerged and are nesting, remove the old blocks for cleaning.

Clean the old blocks by passing a 5/16-inch drill into each hole and shaking out the now pulverized collection of old cocoons, dead bees, unsuccessful larvae, broken mud walls, un-eaten pollen and nectar, and unwanted mites. Attempt to sterilize the holes with a ten percent solution of chlorine water. Now stack the old blocks in your garage to dry for the next season.

Bee raising is surely not rocket science, some people simply drill new nesting holes in the woodpile each spring, or in that old dead cherry tree in the back yard. This rustic method seems to work just fine.

Knox Cellars "System Tubes"

This unique nesting system, like so much of the knowledge about the Orchard Mason Bee, was developed by Dr. Philip Torchio, USDA at the Agricultural Research Station at Logan, Utah. I have improved the design a bit with the development of a small black-plastic end plug. We have adopted this System as the preferred method of propagating and marketing the bee.

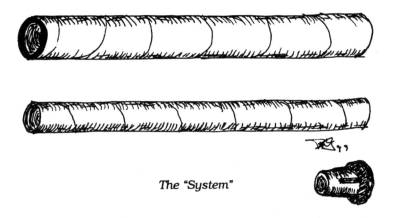

The "System"

The System consists of three simple parts. A thick-walled heavy kraft paper guard tube, a thin-walled white paper inner liner, and the aforementioned plastic plug tapered at just the angle to grasp the liner. Small ridges on the plug bite into the guard tube holding the guard tube and the liner firmly together. The System tubes are six inches long. They are available either in a box of two hundred, or in a cardboard can we call a "Nester." The "Nester" holds seventy-four System tube sets and is ready to install in the garden.

The advantages of the System are several. Of most importance is hygiene. You change the inner liner before you set the bees out for the spring. In October, slip the liners filled with their cocoons of hibernating bees out of the guard tubes and put them in a tin can. Put new clean liners into each guard tube. In the spring set out both the system "Nesters," now empty, and the cans of filled liners. When the bees begin to emerge from the liners they will all go to the clean "Nesters." When they have all emerged, you simply throw the old liners away. With them will go various bacteria, fungal spores, and the odd predator that has overwintered in the bee nesting holes and is waiting to emerge and begin a new cycle of predation.

Before you throw the old liners away be sure you hold them up to the light to see if there are any late emerging bees still in their cocoons. If there are they are likely females and you will want to free them. You can just set them out in a protected warm place and they will usually chew a hole in the cocoon and free themselves. You can also unwind the paper tube to release the cocoon. Then carefully cut a hole in the cocoon and release the bee.

An alternative way to make the annual exchange of soiled for clean paper liners is exceptionally simple. When you think that the last of the females has emerged as evidenced by no more mating activity being observed, simply insert a large wood screw into each soiled hole, catch the paper liner on the screw's threads and draw it off the plastic plug and out of the guard tube. Now as a new clean liner is inserted, it engages the plastic plug and the exchange is complete.

A second advantage of the "System" is the heavy guard tube. The *Monodontomerus* wasp is unable to pierce its sidewalls with its ovipositor. The guard tube saves many bee larvae from an untimely death.

Finally, the System creates a six-inch hole providing the depth at which the optimum number of female eggs are laid. Since females do the great majority of the pollinating, this is a most desirable benefit.

The tubes can be housed in almost anything: waxed milk cartons, seven-inch deep tin cans of many widths, plastic soil pipe, wooden boxes that you might construct. You are only limited by your imagination.

The guard tubes will be usable for many years if you keep them dry. The replacement paper liners are inexpensive and, of course, the plastic end plugs are indestructible. Give the "System" a try.

The "Nester," a circular four-inch diameter cardboard can holds seventy-four of the tube sets. That's enough to house about eight thousand nesting cells. Fill one of these "Nesters" with bees and your apple tree will be very happy.

Soda Straws

I do not recommend using plastic straws for nesting bees; however several resources suggest their use and I continually hear from people who use this method. Let us discuss its merits.

The Orchard Mason Bee may prefer to nest in more absorbent materials, but she will nest in plastic soda straws folded once in the center and stuck into a tin can, cardboard milk carton or any other container. The inside dimension of the straw should be about seven millimeters. Fold each one in half to seal off the back of what are now two nesting holes. When you have folded enough of them to fill your container, bind them together with masking tape so that they will be stable and not spring free.

If possible, fashion a little roof over the front to keep the rain from the hole entrances and mount the trap in some way so that the holes lie horizontally. Use your imagination; the bees won't mind. I have seen soda straws stuck into plastic sewer pipe sections, one half-gallon milk cartons, and rusting tin cans. Anything that will hold the straws and keep them dry will work.

Unfortunately I cannot recommend the use of

plastic straws. The disadvantages of plastic straws are deadly ones. Since they will not absorb moisture they result in a wetter than normal nesting environment which in turn results in fungal and bacterial problems.

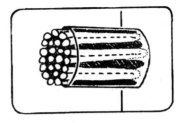

Paper straws, if you can get them, do absorb moisture, as do the wooden nesting holes. They work very nicely except that both types of straws with their thin walls are extremely vulnerable to the depredations of the *Monodontomerus* wasp.

Cardboard Tubes

Some Orchard Mason propagators prefer to place small cardboard tubes in holes specially drilled in a block of wood.

Although I have never used this method, it does provide some interesting advantages. With this method, one can insert new tubes in a block each year. This technique is more hygienic than simply reusing a nesting block in which the bees had nested. Some problems of disease and mite depredation might be reduced. The tubes, with the bees, are removed each fall and can be stored in a spare refrigerator, assuring proper atmospheric and temperature conditions until time to reinsert them in emergence blocks in the spring.

Finally, if your bees are bothered by a parasite that feeds on the spare pollen in the cell, you can unpeel the windings of the tube and collect the hibernating bees in their cocoons. Treat the cocoons for the parasites and then reinsert the cocoons into clean new tubes. A piece of masking tape placed over the tube simulates the mud plug and the parasite-free bees will chew right through it when they are ready to emerge in the spring.

Other Nesting Possibilities

It is well established that the Orchard Mason reproduces in cedar shingle roofs. In fact the native population in my back yard had, for years, been nesting in the shingles of a small garden shed. If you will look carefully at a wood shingle roof, you will notice that the aperture created by two shingles laid side by side on the shingle below is often about 5/16-inch wide. When you lay the next course of shingles, the shingle on top of that aperture creates a square hole of just the right dimensions for a bee nest.

While the bees nest in a horizontal nesting hole, they will also nest in vertical shingle walls frequently found on houses. The slight pitch created by a sloping roof or a vertical hole doesn't bother them at all. In fact I have proof that they thrive in completely upside down nesting holes.

A large number of my breeding stock was trapped last year at a home in Kirkland, Washington. The following story represents the only negative report I have ever heard about the Orchard Mason Bee.

While selling bees at the Northwest Flower and Garden Show in Seattle's convention center, I talked with a couple whom had a bee problem. They listened to my presentation. Afterward they came up to tell me that they didn't need any of my bees; their house was already infested with Orchard Mason Bees.

It seemed that they had recently remodeled their

older home. They had carefully covered the outside walls with cedar shingles. They had placed each shingle the exact distance apart to get the proper shadow effect. You guessed it; the shingles were just 5/16-inch apart. They had created a giant nursery for Orchard Masons.

They had so many bees coming and going across the outside deck each spring that they didn't enjoy eating out, or sitting on the deck. They had hired a pest exterminator to spray the walls but the spray had no effect at all. Next year's bees were all safe behind those shingles and the stout mud walls of the cells. Those nesting holes were of course vertical. The bees entered from below.

There is a happy ending to the story. I offered my assistance and set my fir trap blocks all about their deck. The blocks contained two thousand 5/16-inch holes capable of holding about seven nesting cells each.

I was gratified to find that the bees preferred my nesting blocks to the spaces between the shingles. The majority of the bees nested in my blocks. By the end of the season in June they had filled 1830 of the holes, and I had collected approximately twelve thousand bees. At least twelve thousand fewer bees will be bothering those folks next spring. I will distribute those bees across the country to bring their considerable benefits to home gardeners and fruit growers.

It appears that the size of the hole may be more important than the nesting material. In the urgency of reproductive fervor, our Orchard Mason will build nesting cells in strange places. I have even seen a recorder, a flute-like musical instrument, with a nesting cell plugging its air passage.

A friend recently told me he discovered the reason his outdoor lights were not turning on at dusk and off at dawn this spring. He found that the short tube opening to the light-sensing device was plugged with mud. When digging it out, he was surprised to excavate sweet smelling pollen and nectar. The culprit was, of course, our friendly Orchard Mason who laid her egg in his plastic light sensor. Over the years I have had reports of the bees nesting in rubber compressor hose, aluminum chairs, market umbrellas, and a workbench in the garage. I have experimented with plaster of Paris; I have drilled holes in plastic blocks; I have set out holes in steel, and even a composite of sawdust and paraffin. The bee simply doesn't seem to care. If the hole is the right size it will use it.

Nesting Sites

I have been selling nesting devices and hibernating bees for a number of years now. It has been interesting to observe the propagation success of those nesting devices placed in different sites. I have developed some strong opinions about which kind of sites work the best.

The most successful site I know of is the infested shingle house previously mentioned. It sits about a hundred feet uphill from a large lake. It is surrounded by large trees, although it gets lots of sun from mid-morning on. The trees are native big-leaf maples, a wonderful source of spring pollen. The house is well protected from prevailing winds. Over the ensuing years I have located several other shingle-sided houses that harbor large populations of Orchard Masons. In every case there are big leaf maples nearby and the wall most used by the bees gets lots of sunshine and is protected from the prevailing wind.

Our own propagation site at Knox Cellars is very successful year after year. We generate a six hundred percent population increase in a good year, For each nesting hole with hibernating bees that we set out in the spring we harvest seven newly filled holes by the end of June.

Our nesting devices are mounted on the wall of a small garden shed. The wall fronts on a now unused dog kennel. Ivy and espaliered apple trees grow on the old kennel fence, providing excellent wind protection. Just above the hanging trap nests is the small shingle roof, which not only protects the nests from rain, but also provides a resting and warming surface for the bees. The shingles of this roof were the original nesting place of my colony of bees. We constantly see bees landing briefly on the roof to groom or to warm themselves in the morning.

The nesting holes face south, but the exposure is such that the early morning sun hits them and they are in full sun until early afternoon. In the temperate Western Washington climate the bees never seem to get too hot.

From my observations over the past fifteen years I offer the following suggestions for ideal site criteria:

- Place nests where they will get early morning sun. Let them face east or south, west only if it is your sunniest wall, and never the north wall. Insects are cold blooded and so require

A simple shelter for nesting boxes.

the heat of the sun to get them up to operating temperature each morning.

- Minimize the exposure to wind as best you can. The females carry loads of mud and food that equal a substantial percentage of their body weight; they seek every advantage they can get. If you think you have a wind problem on your sunniest wall you can erect a windbreak for them. Just a board attached to the wall to break the wind will help them.

- Don't hang the nest device in a tree. It is apt to be shaded there; it swings and it is exposed to the wind. The bees will find your fruit trees if their nest is within several hundred feet. Put their home in the sunniest most protected place you can find.

- Don't hang the nest habitat on a fence post out by the apple trees. Over the years countless people have done so thinking to help the poor bees find the blossom. Be assured the bees will find the blossoms. That is why nature equipped them with wings and a keen sense of smell. The bees simply don't like the exposure out there in the open. Take my word for it. They will do best on the sunny wall of a building, under an eave, but far enough down to be in the sun.

The garden house wall in the sun and under the eave.

- If your orchard is three hundred feet from any building and you must site your bees in it, build a simple shelter (as illustrated). You will notice that it provides both wind and rain shelter. Face it toward the sun, and if you have woodpeckers, screen it with chicken wire.

- Locate your nests on the wall of a building. A building acts as a heat sink as warmth of the sun is captured and retained by the building. The bees will do best in the full sun on a building wall, but under an eave that will keep off the worst of the rain. If you have a south-facing wall with an eave, note the shadow line on the wall. Put your bees just below that shadow line.

- Locate your bees where you can enjoy them. They are fascinating to watch and they will not bother you in any way. Too often people hang them too high to see or to tend.

- Mount all of your colony's nesting holes close together. Remember, these bees are gregarious. They don't want space between themselves and their neighbors. The Orchard Masons want to live cheek by jowl, so to speak.

- Don't move the nesting traps around once the bees have emerged. Like the honeybee, the Orchard Mason has a very finely tuned directional sense. If the foraging female leaves on a mission and returns to find that her well-meaning gardener has decided she might enjoy the view better from the rose trellis, the confused lady will simply go looking for another home, perhaps a couple of houses down the block. I have moved nests several times as an experiment. I have switched nests from one side of my colony to another, a distance of perhaps eight feet. The bees return from foraging and cannot find their familiar, hole even though all of the holes and nesting devices are identical to my eyes. The bees hover and land only to take flight again searching in vain for their pheromone-marked hole. They are still searching as my interest wanes and I wander off. Finally after several hours I relent and switch the nest traps back to their original position. Quickly the bees find their own holes and return to a normal behavior pattern.

- Provide moist dirt if you live in an arid climate. First try digging a hole to damp earth. If your area is too arid for that to succeed, go to a river bank and bring home a bucket of clay. Put that on a small piece of plastic in your garden and keep it moist with a watering can from time to time. If that fails just trust to the bee's determination and survival skills. She will probably find a good damp dirt source somewhere in your neighborhood. In my garden I enjoy digging a hole just shovel wide down to the clay that underlies my vegetable garden. It is great fun to watch the parade of bees descending into, and rising, laden, from the "mine" that I have just dug them.

When the bees have finished nesting you can just leave the nesting traps in place on the warm sunny wall until the fall rains begin. The bees can be left outside in all but the most extreme climates. Many people simply raise the habitat up to a nail close under the eave where no winter rain can get to them. I prefer to move my bees to a dry unheated garage where I know they can spend the winter unassailed by marauding woodpeckers or a long sustained sub-zero freeze.

We must be patient, unlike one friend with a "pollinator" who dug out the mud entrance plugs from the nesting holes and then probed the nesting holes with a pipe cleaner, thinking to help the poor bees escape their trap. Needless to say the bees did not survive his well-intentioned ministrations.

Do not winter your bees in a garage attached to the house. Such garages are seldom cold enough. Frequently the furnace is located there. Heat from the house warms it each time the connecting door is opened. It is also too warm in the basement. These bees need cold winter temperatures to successfully hibernate. They will weaken and sometimes die before spring if kept too warm.

Don't worry about brief freezing temperatures. The bees confront freezes in their natural environment and survive nicely. Remember, these bees are natives; they are acclimated to the North American weather. I have seen them nesting at the five thousand foot elevation in the wild mountains of Idaho. Remarkably, the bees develop glycol in their blood which prevents their blood from freezing. They can endure brief freezes; however, if you live in an area with long winter freezes, mortality will increase unless you simulate natural conditions. A bee hibernating deep inside a log, buried under two feet of snow, is insulated from the cold. A bee, hibernating in a 4 × 6 beam, exposed on the apple tree in your back yard to three months of subzero cold, is going to have a tough job of survival. Use your imagination and good judgement. If you are going to leave them outside you might put them in a box with insulation of some kind.

You can also very successfully hibernate your bees in a refrigerator. If this were a perfect world the bees would enjoy a winter spent at thirty-eight degrees Fahrenheit although they adapt nicely to wide swings of temperature. Keeping them in a refrigerator at just above freezing is a good way to winter them both in the extreme frigid north, and in the subtropical states where they are not native because the winters are too warm. You might want to do this if you have a late blooming fruit tree and very few early blossoms to hold the bees in your neighborhood. Japanese orchardists have controlled the emergence of *Osmia cornifrons* in their orchards for many years. They simply refrigerate nesting blocks and warm them up several days before they need bees.

We keep many of our bees refrigerated so that we can extend the season that we can sell and ship them, and we even put "freeze-paks" in our shipment packages late in the shipping season so that the bees don't emerge while in the mail or United Parcel Service truck. We have successfully delayed their emergence until mid-May. That means that the bees will be pollinating through June and into early July.

While you can delay their emergence, there is little you can do to speed them up. There is great impatience each spring among bee fanciers. It seems that you put the bees out on the first of March, and most years you wait and wait. Try not to be impatient with the emerging bees. There is really nothing you can do to help them enter this world. Their emergence is entirely controlled by an age-old stimulus response system that is not entirely understood, but is surely based on temperature.

Some years the bees emerge in late February, and extend their emergence over a number of weeks. In other years they emerge in early April and just seem to burst out of the holes in a period of days. This seemingly erratic emergence pattern is obviously a response to the weather.

In the remarkably warm Puget Sound winter of 1991-92, the bees began emerging in my yard on

February 27th. They continued emerging daily over a long period of time. My observation notes identify March 20th as the first date that I saw a female. This means that males emerged for twenty-three days before a female was identified. The females completed their emergence with more dispatch, but they also came out over at least a ten-day period.

In several locations where sunlight was not sufficient, the start was a good deal later. I had several reports from persons using the "pollinators" that I had sold them of bees nesting even as late as August. I am skeptical of those reports but mention them to illustrate that nature will dictate the timing of the bee's cycle.

It is my standard practice to put my bees and nesting habitat out on the first of March each year. This date is almost always before the bee will emerge, but the *Pieris japonica* is reliably in bloom and the bees will come out when they are ready. They will not be harmed by hanging there on the garden house wall. They will emerge when Mother Nature beckons. It is far better than forgetting about them in the garage during the first spring warm spell. If they emerge there, without new nesting holes, they are sure to perish or disappear, a lost generation.

Nesting Problems

I occasionally get reports that large wasps or other insects are assaulting the sealed-over nesting blocks. While I have never had that problem, it may be a local threat at your home. You might solve the problem by slipping a length of old nylon stocking over the completed nesting device.

Woodpeckers, chickadees and other birds sometimes peck out the protective mud plugs. That challenge can be dealt with simply as well. If using our "Nester" cans, simply turn them around. The birds will see only the bottom of the can. You can also place your nesting devices in a large wooden box and attach chicken wire to the opening. The bees can fly through the mesh but the birds cannot.

Rest assured that the bees' emergence will coincide with the blossoming of their food source. Nature has hooked them into the same temperature/ sunlight wake up signal. Bees and blossoms are interdependent. It could be no other way.

After the eggs are laid and the nesting chambers completed, the bees are subject to serious peril if the nesting traps are handled roughly. Jarring the nesting cells can result in one hundred percent mortality of the eggs and larvae. At the earliest stage a sudden jolt can dislodge the egg from the food provision. The dislodged egg dehydrates and dies.

Even after its hatching, the larva can be easily dislodged from its grip on the cell's food. Unable to climb back to a feeding position, it will die.

Through its entire metamorphosis, with the exception of one month just after cocoon spinning, mortality can be cause by rough handling. It is far safer to leave nesting devices hanging until cool weather in October. By that time each cell will contain a cocoon in which rests an adult Orchard Mason bee sleeping the long sleep until the coming spring. Rough handling won't bother them now. You can move the filled nesting traps very gently if you have a reason to do so at any time after the holes are capped. You might wish to move them out of the traffic of children, or pets, or under rain protection. If you move them be very gentle.

I am occasionally asked by people who are moving to a new home or a new city if they can take their bees with them. The answer is a resounding yes as long as you move them when they are adult and in deep hibernation. That means that you can move them from approximately October 1st to March 1st in my climate. If you must move during the summer you might carefully pack the bees and make arrangements with the new occupant of your house to mail them to you in the fall. Here at Knox Cellars we ship bees to every state with great success.

I mentioned earlier the need for a healthful environment in which to propagate these bees. I speak largely of the use of pesticides in the proximity of the Orchard Mason. If you and your immediate neighbors use pesticides between February and late May, you may create a world in which the Orchard Mason, and most other beneficial insects, cannot survive.

There may be times and places when specific pesticides must be used; however, backyard gardeners can have great success with almost no pesticide use. We have found that we must spray *bacillus thuringensus* in the spring to control the various *lepidoptera* caterpillars, which chomp on our fruit tree leaves. We also spray oil and dormant spray chemicals in late winter to control the scab insects, but beyond that we rely on natural controls.

Over recent years we have come to believe that achieving something of a natural balance is indeed reducing insect damage to the flowers, vegetables and fruit in our garden. At the very least we would rather eat around the occasional insect hole in an apple, than think about the toxic threats of a perfect sprayed fruit.

We believe some of our best allies in the battle against the bad bugs are the chickadees and violet green swallows that nest in our garden. We watched a nesting pair of chickadees in the spring of 1999. We were astonished at the number of little green caterpillars they brought to the birdhouse every day, nay every hour. It made me very happy that I had neglected to do my usual spray of *bacillus thuringensus*. The apple trees don't seem more eaten than those years when I did spray. If I could only guarantee a couple of nesting pairs of chickadees each spring I think I could forget about the spray forever.

We have five birdhouses attached to the various buildings on our city lot.

Two of them are on the north wall of our house. By midsummer, we have a small flock of immature birds searching for bugs all over the garden. Now the truth is that the violet green swallows that nest in the birdhouse just off the bathroom porch surely eat some of my bees. The Peterson bird book "Guide to Birds of North America," lists bees second in the ranking of swallow food favorites. In fact, I recently heard from a customer who has a huge population of nesting barn swallows. He is convinced the birds have wiped out his starting population of Orchard Masons for two years running.

My experience is that the nesting swallows don't arrive in these northern latitudes until April 15th. When they do, the thriving bee colony easily survives the bird depredations. Perhaps the birds catch mostly the elderly males and the depleted females whose time is brief anyway. As the bees work and age, their wings become tattered and they clearly show a reduction in vitality and flight speed. Hopefully it is these weary ones that the swallows find the easiest prey.

By the time the violet-green swallows have hatched their young and are actively feeding them, the bee season is slowing to its end. My final reassurance to you is that insect reproduction rates are extremely high because so many of the Earth's creatures depend upon them for sustenance. The bugs will outbreed their losses to the birds, so invite both of them to your garden.

Many other bird species trade in our yard: crows, jays, starlings, robins, and rosy finches. The reliable attraction is a birdbath made from an old oak wine barrel standing on end. Water drips constantly from the antique brass faucet into the shallow pool formed by the barrel head, keeping the water always fresh.

Each sunny morning the bird bath sounds and looks like a high school swim meet as the birds compete for their turn. I have noticed that if I turn the water off so that it no longer drips, the birds go elsewhere to bathe. They like fresh clean oxygenated water — and who can blame them?

Pesticides can be devastating to the Orchard Mason or any other bee. However, our friend does have several protective advantages over the honeybee. The honeybee foraging on blossoms sprayed with poison can pick the pesticides up on its body and return to the hive where others will groom her. The intimate lifestyle of the honeybee can spread the toxins from bee to bee throughout the hive.

The solitary nature of *Osmia lignaria* offers some protection from toxic sprays. If an individual bee is exposed and survives long enough to get back to the nesting site, the toxins will only affect the health of the cell she is working on. Because she has no contact with other bees, she will not spread the poisons carried on her body. Hopefully, those eggs previously laid and sealed in the nesting chamber will survive to emerge the next spring.

The Orchard Mason lives outside its nesting cell for such a short period of time that if you and your neighbors can refrain from spraying toxic materials until after the foraging season ends, you will kill none of your population of Mason bees. The adults have already died and their work is done. The eggs holding next year's population are safe behind their walls of mud.

Chapter 6

Predators and Parasites

It seems an immutable law of nature that all creatures are prey for some other species. Our Orchard Mason Bee is no exception. In nature's plan a certain percentage of the population of any species becomes dinner for some other species. This remarkable interdependence in the natural world is brutal but it seems to work with a marvelous logic.

The ingenious techniques of the predators, and the unique defenses adopted by the preyed-upon are, for me, the most interesting of nature's wonders. The Orchard Mason bee is prey for a number of predators at all stages of its life. But no time in its life cycle is it more vulnerable than when cloistered in the mud walls of the nesting cell.

Philip Torchio told me recently that to date he has identified 35 nest associates that invade the sanctuary of the Orchard Mason's nest cells. In this chapter we will look at just a few of them. Frequently, concerned bee propagators call me. They have had some of their mud plugs perforated either from within or without by some unknown creature.

Such perforations are never good news as they mean an enemy got within the walls and most likely dined on bees, their larvae or their food. Most likely the invader lived in the cell, evolved to its emergent stage and tunneled its way out without so much as a thank you. My only consolation for people with such problems is to remind them that rarely is the entire colony of bees decimated. The bees will usually out-breed any such depredations.

For ten months and more, the future of the Orchard Mason species depends on the security of those nesting cells. Knowledge of the life history of the bee reveals a host of fascinating adaptations of life that also contribute to the survival of the species.

For instance, why does the female Orchard Mason create two-thirds of her babies as males, and lay those male eggs invariably in the front cells of the nesting chamber? Does she realize, through some primal instinct, that the males are only important for one brief act of copulation, and that only a few must survive until the spring to procreate?

It is the females that assure the survival of the species. They must be protected, so female eggs are laid in the back of the hole. Any predator invading the sanctity of the nesting hole must savage all the males before it gets to the females. Hopefully, spring emergence will occur before the predator eats its way back to the females.

Why does the Orchard Mason construct thin walls separating the nesting cells, but brick up a really thick one at the entrance to the hole? How does she know the first wall is the really important line of defense to keep the barbarians at the gate? Such adaptations help reduce bee mortality. Population loss because of predation is inevitable each year. The Orchard Mason simply has too many enemies to escape some depredation.

In the world outside the nesting cell, birds are probably the worst danger; robins, magpies, and any insect-eating bird will feast on the flying insect. I have observed a pair of red-breasted sapsuckers sitting on a nesting trap picking off the female Orchard Masons as they returned to the nesting holes.

Woodpeckers of many kinds will invade the nesting blocks, looking for succulent larva. I have heard of field mice excavating the nesting holes in search of the hibernating bees.

Depredations by these larger creatures are probably catastrophic when they occur, but they would not be the prime cause of bee mortality. In the natural world, depredation of the nesting cells by their fellow insects takes a greater toll. One of the worst enemies of the Orchard Mason is the *Stelis montana* bee, a member of the same *Megachilid* family. Our friend is not even safe from its close relatives. A tiny wasp represents another serious threat. This wasp plants its eggs on the larva of the Orchard Mason. Its larvae then consume the Orchard Mason larva.

The Orchard Mason is at least pestered by, and I believe damaged by, the tiny pink-colored mite that we mentioned in a previous chapter. We will examine its relationship with the bee.

A variety of marauding beetle larvae and the other nest associates can take their toll on the bees or their larvae, and finally, the bees can suffer mortality from disease and fungal infections.

Despite all these assaults on the population of the Orchard Mason, the bees survive and prosper. Depredation is merely part of the balance that nature has established. The predators and problems seem to control the population but never entirely destroy it. Let's take a closer look at some of these predators. You will want to be able to identify them as you observe your bees.

Mites

 Let us first discuss the parasitic mite. Its name is *Chaetodactylus Krombeini* Baker. This tiny creature thrives in nesting cells where the food provision was not completely eaten by the larva. It is pinkish in color, and is most populous in cells where the egg did not hatch for some reason and the entire food provision did not get eaten. There, the whole food hoard is available to nurture the mites and a teeming population results.

There is some question in the scientific community as to whether the mite kills the egg, thereby freeing all that food for its progeny, or if it simply coexists with the bee, sharing the cell's provisions. Karl Krombein, in his 1962 paper, "Biological Notes on *Chaetodactylus Krombeini* Baker," unequivocally states he has "observed adult mites attacking and feeding on the bee egg and consuming its fluids." He was working with the Eastern Orchard Mason, at Plummers Island, Maryland. Torchio, on the other hand, has tried repeatedly to get the mite to attack the eggs of the western bee without success. In a personal communication, he has told me he cannot state that the mite kills the western bee.

More than a dozen years of observing the bee and splitting open wooden nesting holes or unwinding paper tubes has convinced me that the mites do indeed kill the egg and are a serious threat to the health of a bee colony.

You have already read that the mites cluster on the thorax of the newly emerged bee. It is clear that the mites clamber aboard the emerging bee sometime between when the bee emerges from the cocoon and the time that it leaves the nesting hole.

Periodically, I examine nesting blocks and tubes to try to understand what is going on in the nesting hole. Those examinations indicate that the mites don't live inside the cocoon nor even in a cell containing a cocoon. They are found only in otherwise empty nesting cells in a yellow seething mass of loose granulated food and mites. The egg has disappeared.

Those heavily infested cells are still contained by the stout mud walls that form the cell. It is common to find an infested cell positively teeming with mites, yet the cells both in front and behind will be unaffected. Just as common, when excavating nesting holes, is to find a cell with the food provision intact in a solid, waxy lump of pollen and nectar. There will be no sign of the mites. For one reason or another, the egg failed to hatch and the unused food provision remains in its solid original condition.

I deduce from these observations that the mites cannot pass through cell walls. That they ride into a cell that is being prepared on the back of the nesting female bee, drop off in the cell, and after the cell has been provisioned, the egg laid and the cell closed, the mite or mites attack the egg. The egg is consumed, the food is eaten, and the mites multiply. This mite is capable of reproduction without a sexual partner. A single mite will result in a nesting cell stuffed absolutely full with the mites.

The mites are evident in the cells in October and seemingly live in the cell all winter to emerge in the spring, riding the back of the bee. The bees emerging from cocoons deeper in the hole than the infested mite cell must crawl through it to emerge. The slow crawl through the mite cell gives the mites sufficient time to climb onto the bee, sometimes almost covering the bee with their pink bodies. Once the walls of the cells are pierced, the mites are free to invade all of the cells and wait for the bees to chew out of their cocoons. They quickly climb onto the emerging bees.

Are they biting and eating on the bee or are they simply seeking a ride to new nesting cells to assure that their progeny will have a future? I suspect the latter but I really have no scientific evidence. I am convinced, however, that they kill the eggs.

The bees seem to be successful in scraping the mites off in a day or two, although occasionally I will see a small bee so covered with mites that it appears weakened and unable to rid itself of its distasteful riders. Some of those weakened bees die. The healthy bees will be seen sitting on leaves or the garden house roof, busily scratching off the mites. Soon they are shiny and clean. One wonders if those scraped off mites don't find another Mason bee to climb onto. Perhaps the mites "bail out" over some tempting target to which the bees have flown them. At any rate, in a few days the bees are shiny blue-black and appear to be mite free.

Little is known about the life history of this mite and its relationship with its host. It is apparently not detrimental to the success of the bee unless mite concentrations become too high. The mites don't seem to be a problem in dry mountain country such as the Wasatch mountains of Utah, but are numerous and a threat to colonies in the moist coastal areas of Western Washington and Oregon.

Greg Dickman, in *Orchard Bee* says you can control mites by removing bee cocoons from the nesting holes, immersing them, for five or ten minutes in a solution of water and five percent chlorine bleach. The cocoons are waterproof, thus the bees are not harmed. Any mites on the cocoons are killed. Then you must replace the cocoons into a nesting hole, or a straw, finally plugging the entrance with a small wad of cotton.

The writer suggested the importance of aligning all replaced cocoons, "nipple" end toward the entrance. He correctly wants to avoid starting the bee in the wrong direction during spring emergence.

I have tried Dickman's bleach method without success. I found that a five percent bleach solution did not kill the mites, but it did begin to dissolve the cocoons so that I hurriedly had to rinse them off with clear water. I found the mites to be very tough indeed. I even scraped a few mites into a ceramic saucer and put them in the microwave oven.

I figured a couple of minutes in the microwave would be sure death. Not so. They needed more time. Of course you can't put bee cocoons in a microwave. The bees would pre-decease the mites.

I believe the best control technique is to destroy last years emptied nesting holes. The idea is to keep the mite population at a low number by destroying each year's left-over population.

Before we leave the subject of mites, let me point out that these *Chaetodactylus* mites are not the mites that have ravaged the European honeybee in North America. There are many thousands of different species of mites on this Earth. They have very specific life histories which allows each species to thrive only in a narrow band of supporting environment.

The varroa mite and the tracheal mite that are victimizing the honeybees affect only the honeybee. The native bees of North America do not face their threat because their lifestyles do not support those two species of mites.

Stelis montana

This bee predator is a member of the same *Megachilidae* family the Orchard Mason belongs to. It victimizes a number of the *Megachilid* bees, including *Osmia californica* and *Osmia montana* mentioned previously.

The *Stelis* female patrols the Orchard Mason nesting site, flying ten to fifteen centimeters in front of the nesting blocks. Finding a likely nesting hole that has not yet been completed, she lands at the entrance and directs her sensitive antennae into the hole. Is she checking for a protective mother Orchard Mason, or is she somehow learning whether or not the nesting cell is still open?

If her inspection is favorable, she enters and deposits her egg in the partially prepared food provision. She always takes care to lay her egg at some distance from the spot that the Orchard Mason will eventually lay her egg.

The *Stelis* initiates flight at a warmer temperature than the Orchard Mason. The marauding female is usually on patrol at least an hour after the Orchard Mason has started work. By the time *Stelis* becomes active, our Orchard Mason mother has had time to gather enough food to provision a cell but not to seal it up — just what the *Stelis* wants. Sometimes several *Stelis* females will each lay an egg in the same cell. Thus there will be more than one parasite in the cell when it is sealed.

The hard working female Orchard Mason returns with a fresh load of nesting materials, not knowing that there is one or several intruders in her nest who will eventually slay her offspring. She completes the nest cell and seals it up, unaware of the danger.

Stelis eggs are small in relation to the host egg — approximately two millimeters, rather than the three and four-tenths millimeter of the Orchard Mason. They are nearly straight or only slightly curved. In about five days they enter the embryo stage, then the larval stage, and by the time they have progressed to the fifth larval stage they are mobile. The first act of the *Stelis* larva is to kill its competition. If there is another *Stelis* larva in the cell, it is attacked and killed but not eaten.

Attention is then turned to the large Orchard

Mason larva. It too is assassinated, but unlike the dead *Stelis* larva, this meal is tempting. The juices are sucked from the punctured carcass by the surviving *Stelis*. When the larva has been consumed, baby *Stelis* now turns to the pollen and nectar supply. After eating its fill the *Stelis* larva spins its cocoon. There it will complete its maturing process, sleep away the winter, and re-emerge the following spring.

The *Stelis* spends the winter in a pre-pupae stage, molting into the pupa during the emergence state of the Orchard Mason. It rapidly completes its metamorphosis, and by the time the Orchard Mason is at the peak of its egg-laying activity, the now adult *Stelis montana* chews out of its cocoon and emerges. Three or four days later, it has mated, and is patrolling the nesting sites, ready to do its dirty deed to another generation of Orchard Masons.

Stelis montana sounds like a deadly threat that would destroy every last *Osmia* bee, but nature is more clever than that.

Remember, *Stelis* emerges after our Orchard Mason is at the peak of egg laying, three or four more days are spent feeding and mating, and by the time the *Stelis* female starts her deadly work, there are lots of nesting cells completed, safe from her depredations.

Even better, most of the female eggs have been laid in those early cells. The *Stelis* predator kills a lot of bees, but does not really damage the population of *Osmia* bees because it kills mostly the males. Fortunately, its larvae do not invade adjoining cells. They cannot break through the mud walls.

Torchio's study shows that of cells invaded by

Stelis forty-eight percent were the outermost cell, 20.9 percent in the second cell, and 15.1 percent in the third cell. That means that eighty-four percent of all *Stelis* damage was done to the three outermost cells. Nature has sacrificed the males by having the mother bee lay male eggs in the front cells of the nesting hole. The species survives.

Monodontomerus Wasps

These tiny *Chalcid* wasps are the most serious parasite of the Orchard Mason Bee. The wasps invade the bee nesting cells only after the cocoon is spun. They touch their sensitive antennae to the wood of the nesting block to detect the movements of the larvae or pupae within the cell. When they detect movement, they insert their ovipositor through the wood, into the cell, through the cocoon to lay an egg upon the larva or pupa within. The egg hatches and the wasp larva, now comfortably within the chamber of the bee, slowly eats away the bee larva — a grisly but successful way to make a living indeed.

The wasp larva, having consumed its host, hibernates, and emerges from the commandeered bee nesting hole the next year, just in time to assault another generation of Orchard Mason cocoons. These wasps are most damaging when Orchard Mason eggs are laid in thin walled nesting holes such as plastic or paper straws or hollow plant stems. The ovipositor is capable of easily piercing the thin walls and planting the egg inside the cocoon. Dr. Torchio tells me that indeed the *Monodontomerus* can penetrate wood up to three quarter the length of its long ovipositor.

It was for this wasp pest that the Knox Cellars nesting "System" was especially developed. This spring I was cutting open late cocoons and releasing females who had not yet emerged. I was intrigued to find a number of cocoons, each containing six or seven of these wasp assassins still in their pupal form. It was obvious to me that the *Monodontomerus* lays more than five and less than eight eggs each time she invades a cocoon, that the wasps overwinter as pupae, completing the final stage of the metamorphosis just days before emergence.

It was also evident that they do not emerge until late in the season after the Orchard Masons have done much of their nesting and the cocoons have been spun. That delayed timing explains why I have never seen them in my nesting sites until the last half of the season. It would not be to their advantage to emerge until Orchard Mason nesting is well along.

If you are able to get access to a microscope, as mentioned in the final chapter, make every effort to capture and look at one of these miniature wasps. Only three or four millimeters (less than 1/4 inch) long, the *Monodontomerus* is incredibly beautiful and graceful. Its body is mostly a shimmering metallic green accented with legs of yellow ochre. Its jewel-like appearance is enhanced by its intricate architecture.

Be sure to note the ovipositor sheath which protrudes from its rear. You will see that its function is protection and support for the ovipositor, which lies folded up under the wasp's abdomen. With a pin try to fold out the ovipositor. You will not believe its length. The thought that a structure small and strong enough to pierce wood and pass an egg through it, could also be foldable staggers my imagination.

Watch for this little killer cruising your nesting blocks in early June.

Other Wasps

Perhaps this is the place to discuss those hunting relatives of the bee, the wasps. Not as enemies of the Orchard Mason, because only the *Monodontomerus* wasp is; but as interesting and important bee relatives.

If bees are peaceful gatherers in nature's garden, the wasps are the silent hunters. They must hunt and kill or capture to supply the meat upon which their larvae depend. Many or most adult wasps, like the bees, feed on rich nectar to provide the energy for survival but, unlike the bees, they are carnivores in the larval stage.

Unfortunately wasps have developed a bad name amongst the unknowing, largely because of that common pest, the yellow jacket. Yellow jackets, *Vespula vulgaris*, a social wasp, breed large populations in complex nests in the ground or in the walls of buildings. They are highly attracted to meat and fish and anything with sugar in it and thus become annoying pests at summer picnics and barbecues. They are aggressive and quick to anger as most North Americans can attest.

I make but two pleas on behalf of the wasps. First, don't call them bees. Make the effort to learn the difference and distinguish between these two important families bees and wasps, as you speak.

Second, please realize that there are approximately fifteen thousand different species of wasps in North America. Without them we would be overrun by other insects, for the wasps are the great hunters of the insect world. Most of them are specialists, they feed their larvae the meat of only one family of insect victims. Some hunt only one species of insect. Some wasps are spider hunters, others prey only on beetles, or grasshoppers, or caterpillars. Most of them are solitary creatures and pose no threat to mankind, the beneficiary of their diligent bug reduction activities.

Allow me to introduce you to a lovely beneficial wasp that shares my garden, and probably yours. Its genus name is *Passaloecus* and it feeds its young only aphids that it hunts among my apples and flowers. *Passaloecus* is tiny, only 3/8-inch long. It is entirely black and sports the typical "wasp waist."

I first met this busy hunter one day when I noticed that the little 1/8-inch holes in one of our observation houses were all plugged with what appeared to be tree pitch. When I examined the viewing chamber I found to my amazement three nest cells, separated by the same clear pitch-like material, and each cell completely stuffed with aphids.

A little reading and a couple of phone calls to prominent entomologists who specialize in wasps and my introduction to *Passaloecus* was complete. This tiny hunter, completely harmless to man, feeds its larvae only live aphids. It cruises about the garden until it spots the prey. Landing upon it, the wasp carefully stings the aphid in the nerve center at the top of the thorax.

The aphid is quickly paralyzed, not killed. The wasp carries the comatose victim to its tomb, the nesting cell. Thrown into the cell with sixty or seventy other helpless creatures, the aphid waits. When enough aphids have been collected, the wasp lays her egg amongst them and hurriedly seals them all in, using pitch gathered from a nearby tree. After a couple of days the wasp egg hatches and the grisly carnage begins. One by one the larva eats the waiting but paralyzed victims. Each day the larva grows, until finally, when the last aphid is eaten, the now large, spotted grey larva rests briefly before beginning its metamorphosis which will eventually result in another adult wasp out in the garden hunting aphids.

Think twice when spraying your garden to kill insects. You may be killing *Passaloecus* and other valuable allies.

Tricrania Stansburyi

This beetle is a parasite of several *Megachilid* bees throughout western North America. A second species of *Tricrania* is widely distributed in the eastern United States and is a parasite of at least three bees on that side of the country. The adult beetles of both species are similar in appearance. They are black, with blood red wing-covers, and measure six to ten millimeters in length. Strangely, the eastern species is flightless, while the western insect has developed wings.

The beetle has been a known predator of the Orchard Mason for many years. Because its depredations were minor in all previous studies, the beetle's biology has not been extensively studied. However, in 1989 and 1990 the rates of its parasitism rose in two locations in Utah from the expected one or two percent, to fourteen percent and thirty-three percent, respectively. A closer look at this creature was justified.

The *Tricrania stansburyi* life cycle begins in the nesting cell of a host bee. The adult beetles emerge in the spring with the emerging bees, and immediately, courtship and mating begin. A female will frequently mate with several males, but soon it loses interest and flies off to look for a plant to lay its now viable eggs upon.

Two or three days after emergence, *T. stansburyi* lays its cluster of eggs, but only on certain selected plant species. Each female lays an average of four hundred eggs, bound together by a sticky substance secreted by the beetle. On the seventh or eighth day after being laid, the rapidly developing eggs split open to release the *triungulin,* or first larval stage.

The *triungulins* look a little like miniature earwigs with pinchers on the front rather than rear. The larvae are long and thin with prominent mandibles and a forked tail. They are mobile, with short legs, and are attracted toward light so they crawl upward toward the sun. They climb and climb on their pre-selected plant, until they reach the top level, the blossom. There they arch their backs upward and wave their mandibles whenever a stranger passes by.

You have already guessed the rest of the story, I suspect. A foraging bee lands on the blossom and brushes its hairy leg over the waiting *triungulin.* Snap! The mandibles close over a fine hair on the bees leg, and the *triungulin* hangs on for the ride of its life. The unsuspecting bee flies back to the nesting cell with its load of pollen and nectar. As soon as it enters the cell, the *triungulin* lets go of the bee hair.

The bee, frequently an Orchard Mason, seals up the nesting cell, unaware that her recently laid egg is doomed. The *triungulin* gets right to work. If, by chance, several *triungulins* rode in on the same bee, mortal combat ensues immediately. The victor then attacks the freshly laid egg, piercing it with its re-curved mandibles. For several days it feasts on the juices of the egg until the egg case is empty. Then the *triungulin* turns to the pollen and nectar supply.

Strangely enough, the *triungulin* cannot survive in a cell with only pollen and nectar and no egg. It apparently must eat the egg to get itself to the next stage, at which it can then eat the pollen and nectar. Additionally, two *triungulins* introduced to a cell with no egg, pollen, or nectar will not initiate combat but will die of starvation.

The victorious *triungulin*, having dined on the egg and secure in the bee cell surrounded by rich pollen and nectar, need only eat and grow and evolve. Soon, its metamorphosis is complete, and like the host bee, it enters a state of torpor. All fall and winter it sleeps in the cell awaiting the spring and the renewal of its life cycle.

This story must end by reporting that the thirty-five percent parasitism rate reported earlier was explained by Philip Torchio's study: 1989 and 1990 were drought years in Utah. The wild flowers favored by the Orchard Mason, in the particular desert canyon studied, did not bloom well. The bees were forced to forage on a secondary flower choice, one favored by *T. stansburyi.* Had they been able to use their traditional flowers, the parasitism rate probably would have stayed at one percent.

Other Enemies

Among the other creatures that victimize the Orchard Mason are a cocoon wasp *(Leucospis)* and a carpet beetle *(Anthrenus verbasci)* that are attracted to opened cells and old nests. The larvae of the carpet beetle are capable of digging through the mud dividing walls and can thus destroy all the bees in a nesting hole.

There is also a large yellow and black solitary wasp that competes with the Orchard Mason for nesting holes. They hunt small caterpillars and are actually a beneficial insect, but they will damage the *Osmia lignaria* cells as they emerge by tearing down the walls. If this wasp is nesting in your colony you can identify its finished cells because it carefully smooths the surface of the mud plug, whereas the Orchard

Mason entrance plug is always rough.

The Orchard Mason shares one health threat with the honeybee, chalkbrood. This fungal affliction was first reported in Europe in 1944. It was found in the New World by Baker and Torchio in 1968. By 1974 thirty-five states had confirmed its presence. Chalkbrood has become a major problem for commercial honeybee producers. The fungus, *Ascophaera Torchioi*, afflicts both the honeybee and the Orchard Mason.

You can recognize chalkbrood if you open a nesting hole and find cells containing partially completed cocoons that are dry and brittle and contain round black fungal organisms. Apparently chalkbrood only affects one or two percent of healthy Orchard Mason colonies and is not considered the threat that it poses to honeybee colonies

Alarming as all these predators, parasites, and diseases seem, they are all part of the marvelous balance that nature has established. The predators control the population but never entirely destroy it.

The Orchard Mason has survived in North America for millions of years. Have faith that it will continue to thrive in the face of its enemies and make a home in your back yard.

Our advice would be to watch with curiosity the depredations of these various insects. Don't interfere unless your Orchard Masons seem to be seriously threatened.

Chapter 7

Fun With Bees

If you decide to propagate the Orchard Mason for yourself, beware! You will be opening the door to a new world of activity. Your curiosity may lead you to all sorts of projects and interests that you had never anticipated. Some of your friends might begin to discuss you behind your back. Even your family may begin to apologize for your strange behavior.

I speak from experience, but without apology, for I have found great joy in my fascination with the Orchard Mason. Perhaps you will wish to try some of the following tips for having fun with your bees.

Make an Observation Box

Most springs I install several observation boxes in my colony. They are easy to make and allow me to see in great detail and clarity the completed nesting cell. There is the food pile, pollen and nectar, piled in a golden hoard. Implanted in it is the shimmering egg. I have watched the egg become a larva, the larva eat the food and, finally, spin itself into its silken cocoon.

I have seen the carefully constructed masonry walls, and the thick entrance plug. Hopefully, in the spring, I will watch the bees awaken and work their way out to the sunshine.

The observation block is a wonderful tool to get children excited about nature. Children and adults alike look intently at the orderly cell construction and the life within, and they begin to understand what you have been telling them about the life history of the Orchard Mason. If a picture is worth a thousand words, peering into the secret chamber of the bee nest is even better. Some of the notes of my observation file might illustrate.

June 24th, 1992: *Today the #1 larva spun its cocoon. In twenty-four hours it is completely encased and the cocoon is attached to the sides of the chamber. The nipple facing the anterior end is prominent and obvious. Pretty amazing.*

June 27th, 1992: *This day the larva in cell #2 began to spin. With one end immobile, the anterior end extended and traced the outline of the cocoon, spinning with invisible threads. Only after some time did the accumulation of threads begin to obscure the outline of the larva. The next morning the larva was encased and not visible behind the light colored cocoon. I presume the spinning continues for some time inside an ever thickening cocoon. The*

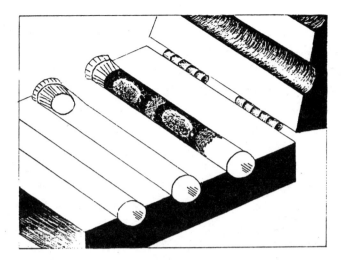

cocoon darkens in color over a period of several days, either because of the increasing thickness or because the threads are exposed to the atmosphere.

Now the long nine-month wait as the metamorphosis continues behind that opaque brown cocoon. I expect to watch in the spring, as the wakened bees answer nature's summons to the daylight.

All this is possible because the bees will lay eggs in a glass tube. Here is how you can do it.

Clamp two perfectly flat pieces of wood tightly together. Then drill directly down the joint line, separating the blocks and creating a hole which is half drilled in each block of wood. Insert into each hole a small glass tube with an inside diameter of seven millimeters, or 5/16-inch. The tubes can be found at bead or craft stores or at chemistry supply houses. Secure the tube in one block with a spot of epoxy glue, or a thin copper wire. Plug one end of each tube with a piece of wooden dowel. The tubes must be tightly plugged at the back or the bees won't use them. They apparently know that predators can enter the back door unless it is well sealed.

Now all that you need do is attach two small hinges and some sort of a closing latch. A hook and eye will do. You can even hold the two halves of the box together with rubber bands.

If you don't have the tools or the inclination to make your own observation block, Knox Cellars sells a very clever model that has three different size holes, each visible through a clear sheet of acetate. Each size will interest a different bee species.

Now you are ready to hang the observation block with your other nesting traps in the hope that a bee will use it. I would encourage you to have the observation block ready at the very first of the season when you hang your other nesting holes out. The bees are less inclined to use these glass or plastic enhanced nest holes, and you want to give them the opportunity when they are fresh and eager.

Keep an Observation Journal

There is much to be learned about the Orchard Mason Bee and its propagation. I strongly suggest that you take observation notes as you watch this fascinating creature. Doing so will increase your enjoyment, heighten your powers of observation, and teach you a great deal about the bee as the years go on.

In 1992 I began recording bee observations on my computer when the mood struck. I have found those notes to be valuable in review. Here are some excerpts from my note book.

March 4th, 1992: *The bees are emerging rapidly this morning. I stand at the blocks and watch their heads first appear at the holes, then widen their hole in the mud wall, and finally squeeze through to freedom. It's pretty exciting as several can be seen at once. When they get out many of them drop to the ground and groom their wings. Then they fly off. Already some return to the breeding blocks and even re-enter the holes for a brief period as though they recognize the holes as home base.*

At emergence the bees have a russet patch of what looks like thick hair on the back of their thorax. It will be interesting to see if that disappears with age. The bees seem to all be males. Not shiny at emergence. Several that have flown back to the blocks are quite shiny.

March 22nd, 1992: *The bees at emergence have a russet red, granular substance all over their thorax. They rub it off after a day or two and thereafter are bright and shiny. I first thought it was a hair covering of some sort, but the past few days I've been thinking it might be a parasite. A mite perhaps, because around several of the nesting holes I see a mass of similar colored substance which in heavy concentrations seems to move.*

Surely what I am seeing on the blocks is a mite of some sort. Can it be possible that they share the nesting hole with some sort of beneficial mite that covers their thorax at emergence? I called an ac-

quaintance in Bellevue to test my theory. He would have none of it, assuring me that the red covering was to keep them from freezing in the nesting hole.

March 23rd, 1992: *About three days ago I began seeing the females. Prior to that time I had been intently looking at males and trying to see a female. Once you see the females there is no mistaking them. They are MUCH larger; they buzz when they fly with a loud and bee-like sound. Their antennae are about half as long as the males'. They are already laying eggs and building nesting chambers. Their flights are purposeful — frequently direct to the hole, in, out and on about their business, a great contrast to the males that flit from place to place with lots of frantic circling and chasing. The males are obviously obsessed with mating. They fly up and "hit" other males, sitting for a moment in the sun, then fly away to "hit" another. Apparently they are looking for females. When they see a black insect they dive at it and "hit" it but, I assume, immediately realize it is of the wrong sex or species and so bounce off and look for another. Occasionally they mount another male briefly until they discover their error.*

March 24th, 1992: *Today I made a rather exciting discovery. The russet, red coating on the thorax of the newly emerging bee is in fact a mass of tiny microscopic mites of some kind. I had placed a newly emerged female in the observation box last night. I was interested in how long it would take her to scrape off the red coating, and how long be-*

fore her wings would open and she would take flight. At lights out last night the coating was covering the back of her thorax. This morning, before she stirred from the crevice she had spent the night in, and before she became active, I checked her.

Some of the red substance had moved to the top of her wings. Aha!! My earliest suspicion that the red stuff was in fact a living organism took on more credence.

Later this afternoon I found a newly hatched female on the courtyard bricks. She had been slightly mangled by a passing shoe. Her ardent suitor had been squished. I picked her up and took her to the shop, found my tiny penlight magnifier and scraped some red stuff onto a piece of white paper. It was soon apparent that I was dealing with something alive. The tiny gob of red stuff separated into tiny, barely visible specks that moved across the paper.

Faced with a rampant curiosity, I went to visit a neighbor who owns an excellent microscope. We soon had the mystery solved. The back of the bee was infested with a mass of ugly little pink mites, all moving legs and what looked like antenna or cilia. When placed on paper they crawled rather rapidly around. An ugly mass of bug to say the least.

Now to find out what they are. I conclude that they are some sort of symbiotic insect which shares the bee's nesting chamber and does some service for him in return for a benefit received. What benefit that might be I have no idea. For the present I will assume they are not harmful. My Bellevue acquaintance has them on his bees in Bellevue. I would bet all Orchard Mason Bees have them.

It will be fascinating to learn just what they are and what they do for the relationship.

Emergence; not a lot of new holes opened today. I think only two, but I saw at least four new females. All of them on the ground, with immature wings,[1] being mated by an eager male. In one case the male was also covered with the red mites. Is it possible that the male and female emerged from the same or neighboring holes and immediately began copulating upon getting outdoors? As aggressive and desperate as the older males appear, one would think they would find and mount the females first.

The females at emergence are slow, with wings that appear underdeveloped, and laden with mites. Most of them seem to fall to the ground to get limbered up and cleaned off, only to be found and mounted by a lusty male. It may be nature's way of getting them bred before they are too mobile. The females must grow after emergence, as the ones I have been seeing on the ground are a good bit smaller than the great, fat-bellied ladies that are so busily working the nesting blocks.[2]

March 29th, 1992: *The spring weather continues warm and sunny. Each day for the last six or seven days I have seen new females emerging. They frequently come out of a hole and are immediately mounted by a hovering male. When another male piles on, the weight of two males causes the female*

---

1. I was wrong, the wings were mature but damp.
2. I later learned that adult bees don't grow. These bees were damp from the cocoon. As their hairs dried they appeared larger.

to let go, and all three of them fall to the ground where the copulation continues. In one instance I saw a female's head emerge, immediately a male pounced, trying to pull her out of the hole. She pulled out of his grasp and retreated backwards into the hole. The male followed her in. After a bit the female emerged and right behind her was the male who instantly mounted her as they got out of the hole. He had crawled past her, turned in the hole and drove her out with his attentions.

There continues to be a significant size differential in bees, both male and female. There are several males so small that they appear to be a separate miniature species. They are half the size of the average male but appear to be Orchard Masons in every respect. Some of the females are really huge, with nicely rounded abdomens and a healthy bee buzz when flying. The females, when they emerge are noticeably smaller than those working the nests. I would surmise that they grow in all dimensions upon emergence. Surely being bred and filling with eggs has a lot to do with the growth.[3]

April 5th, 1992: *The weather has remained at record warm temperatures until yesterday. This morning at 10:30 AM the thermometer on the garden house shows fifty-five degrees. The females are working, although at a slower pace than on a good day. Numbers of them are visible at the hole entrances as though they are waiting for a little better*

---

3. Wrong again. Bees don't grow after emergence. Their hard exoskeletons are formed as the final act of their metamorphosis. They cannot change size after that.

temperature, or they are soaking up enough heat from the wood block for their next foray after nesting materials.

The blocks continue to fill at a satisfying pace. I have one block drilled with 1/4-inch holes and just a dozen 5/16-inch holes. The smaller holes have definitely filled faster than the larger holes, although when watching the bees I have the sense that the same proportion of bees are going to each sized hole.

Perhaps it is simply easier for them to fill the smaller holes because of the smaller volume and so they do it more rapidly.

Whether or not the percentage of females is higher in the larger holes, one compelling reason to switch to 5/16 inch is to avoid expanding wood fibers from sealing up the smaller 1/4-inch hole. It seems that if the wood is fairly soft, the fibers expand with outdoor moisture.

Another factor surely must be the sharpness of the drill bit. If it is dull some fibers will be bent and not cut. When moistened they straighten and plug the hole. A very sharp brad point drill bit will be the best. All things considered, I am convinced that the 5/16 hole is the best bet.

April 6th, 1992: *Today I had big news. I again called for Dr. Dan Meyer at the Washington State U. extension office at Prosser. I finally got him on the phone. He assured me that the mites were no big deal. A common and symbiotic rider on Orchard Mason Bees. They are not a problem unless they get so thick that they can stunt the bees' wings. I guess I have no problem after all, for which I am* *grateful and relieved.*

April 30th, 1998: *I just counted the garaged bees in the dog kennel with a flashlight. I counted 454 females and may have missed about twenty. Almost every unfilled hole has a bee in it and so I hung three more 78-hole nesting blocks.*

We are enjoying a very warm week and now, just at the peak of bee activity they are filling holes at an amazing rate. The temperature is rising to the 70s. Almost record temperatures for the end of April. If this keeps up it will be a wonderful bee crop. Another three days and the first sixteen 78-hole nesting blocks will be filled, plus about 240 of our new "System" tubes that are six inches deep. That totals a lot of bees for next spring.

I have, for the first time, dug a narrow hole down to clay in the center of the vegetable garden. Within twenty minutes a constant stream of bees was coming and going down into and up from the hole. It looks like King Solomon's mine with little black miners excavating side tunnels following a vein of damp clay laterally. At any one time, in the peak of the day, there are probably twenty bees in the hole digging and loading up. It is a fun thing to do and surely increases the efficiency of the bees as it decreases the energy they must expend in nesting. A worthwhile tip to pass along.

I saw the first of the emerging Osmia coreulscens yesterday. There are still a few male O. lignaria about, pestering the females.

May 8th, 1999: *Yesterday I had a new learning experience. I still had about thirty tubes of bees in* the refrigerator. On April 29th, suspecting that the bees had been kept in refrigeration too long to remain viable, or were too close to emergence to be able to ship, we ceased any further sales for the year. I put the remaining tubes outside in my bee colony to release them if they would emerge. After nine days most of the entrance plugs had been perforated and I assumed that the bees were out and hard at work. I was curious why three or four of the tubes had plugs that had not been penetrated and so yesterday I decided to examine their contents before throwing the tubes into the garbage can.

One of the great advantages of using the "System" tubes quickly asserted itself. It is a simple matter to slip the liner containing the bee cells out of the protective guard tube and to peel the liner straw back along its spiraling wrap lines to reveal what has been going on with the bees. The tubes with still intact plugs revealed live males still chewing away at the thick protective plug separating them from freedom. They were all out of their cocoons and stacked up at the entrance plug either working at release or too weary to complete the penetration of the plug. When released by the peeled away paper they immediately shook the debris of mud wall and shredded cocoon from their hairy bodies and gratefully flew off to a waiting blossom to sate their appetites.

At the back of the tubes the unwinding spiral of paper revealed cocoon after large cocoon, unopened and presumably holding bees, either dead or alive. May 8th is extremely late in the season for Western

Washington bees to be emerging. It is a full thirteen months after most of the eggs had been laid the previous year. They should have urgently chewed their way through the cocoons by now. Each of the unopened nesting tubes told the same story. Live males waiting behind the thick plug, large unopened cocoons toward the back of the tube.

Bees in hibernation have metabolisms that slowly consume the food reserves in the bee's bodies. If left in the refrigerator too long, the bees simply starve to death.

With this thought in mind I turned to the remainder of the tubes, those that had perforated entrance plugs indicating that bees had emerged. One after another the peeling spirals of paper revealed the same story. Front nesting cells and cocoons opened and chewed into debris, large unopened cocoons between intact cell walls toward the backs of the tubes. As I peeled tubes I saved these unopened cocoons in a little pile until I had accumulated perhaps twenty-five of them. Then, my curiosity could not be put off any longer. I went into the workshop, returning with a sharpened jackknife and a pair of tweezers.

I stood at the potting bench under the still blooming Pieris japonica and began to carefully open cocoons by cutting a small rent in the tough wall with the knife blade held cutting edge up, and cutting along the axis of the cocoon so as to cut just the enveloping cocoon and not the bee within. When a small opening was made, I carefully slipped one tong of the tweezers into the hole, pointed along the length of the cocoon. By clamping the tweezers firmly, the cocoon fabric was held tight. It was then an easy matter to re-insert the sharp knife blade and slice along the cocoon. By the time the tweezers were inserted, the cocoons held between the tips of the fingers of my left hand were vibrating and buzzing. When the rent on the cocoon was large enough, a thoroughly awakened and active female bee would crawl out into the sunlight.

I carefully placed each bee on the Pieris blossoms just over my head. Cocoon after cocoon was opened and each revealed a large, healthy and active female, some of which immediately flew from my hand to freedom. I was fascinated and perplexed. Why had these seemingly strong females not emerged on their own in the nine days outdoors in the bee colony? I had placed the tubes in the sun, and while we have had cool nights and not the best of weather in these recent days, there have been many afternoons of sunshine and very pleasant weather. They should have emerged.

Had I kept them in the refrigerator just too long so that they had weakened to the point that they could not chew through that tough cocoon? Would they have died in those tubes had I not done my Cesarean surgery? Whatever the answer to these questions, I was delighted to add these late arrivals to the bee population in my colony, some of whom were already worked out and dead. Would this be a way to force mason bees into a longer pollination period? It will be interesting to see if this sizable infusion of females will be working through June and into July long after naturally emerged bees have died.

Intrigued I opened and peeled every one of the nesting tubes. I carefully cut open every cocoon I found. Somewhere after forty-five I lost track of the number of lovely black female bees that I had released. I think the number was about sixty bees that were put into circulation. Enough to pollinate a quarter acre of an apple orchard.

The benefits of my efforts did not stop at releasing bees for I found some interesting surprises in the cocoons. Five or six cocoons held dead and hardened bee larvae that had died shortly after spinning the cocoon around themselves. The cause of their demise was not evident.

Of a great deal more interest were the occasional cocoons that held five or six small white larvae, of some creature. I speculated that they were Monodontomerus wasps in a suspended stage of metamorphosis. I presumed that they would soon recommence metamorphosis and complete their development into the tiny adults which prey on the Orchard Mason. I had opened four or five of these violated cocoons, wondering about the identity of the occupants when I finally opened a cocoon whose sole occupants were five or six tiny adult wasps.

They were dead, but their identity was clear: the Monodontomerus. These wasps had apparently completed their metamorphosis but were unable to get out of the cocoon. Perhaps the cold temperature of the refrigerator had killed them. To prove my thesis, I have placed several of the cocoons containing the mysterious pupae in a small plastic bottle. When they complete the metamorphosis to adulthood we will know for sure what the mysterious intruders are. If they are the wasp that I suspect, I will have a new understanding of the intertwined cycles which these tiny assassins share with the Orchard Mason.

Each spring midway through the active period for the bees I see significant numbers of the Monodontomerus appear before the nesting holes. Sometimes they rush into the nesting hole when mother bee leaves it on a provisioning run. Mostly they are walking about the nesting blocks, twitching their antenna as though hunting for something. Of course they are hunting — for a juicy bee larvae, which has spun its cocoon and is resting inside before continuing its development into an adult. If the wasp can find the opportunity, she will insert her long ovipositor through wood or paper, into the nesting cell and, of course, into the cocoon. Through the hollow ovipositor she will then pass six or seven eggs. Those eggs develop into larvae.

The wasp larvae eat the bee larva and soon the wasps are all alone in the cocoon to wait through the winter, mature into adulthood and emerge right in the center of the busy Orchard Mason nesting colony. I presume they always wait emergence until the bees have had time to prepare waiting cocoons and larvae, otherwise they would have nothing to prey upon.

If the wasps emerge only after all of the bees have emerged it follows that one of the control techniques would be to destroy all old nesting blocks and tubes when I am sure that the female bees have emerged. Burning those old nesting blocks or tubes will eliminate the wasps awaiting maturation in the invaded cocoons. In addition, mites and various fungal growths and bacteria thrive in the old nesting holes. Burning those used nesting holes would assign many of these little killer wasps to the fiery furnace.

I hope that the foregoing sample of my "Observation Notes" hints at the excitement of learning that I have so enjoyed with these bees. There is much that science doesn't yet understand in the life and nature of these creatures. Your experiences, duly recorded in notes of some kind, could make a contribution to man's understanding of the wild bees. At the very least such notes provide a record of when things occurred in the past, so you can have some idea of what to expect in the future.

Bee Watching

Observation of these busy little pollinators is a great pleasure for children. There is enough activity at the nesting sites that my active preschool grandchildren would sit on my knee watching for amazing periods of time. A bee's foraging round trip is of short duration. I sometimes placed a pencil mark below a hole that is being used and we would watch for that particular bee to return.

There was great excitement when the bee returned to her hole. Then it was important to see if we could spot the yellow pollen on the bottom of her abdomen. If she was bearing pollen, we could usually see her yellow bottom just as she scuttled into the hole. Now those grandchildren are older and have become astute observers of the natural world around them. I would like to think that it is partially because of our watching the Mason bees together.

Perhaps the greatest fun for kids is counting the nesting females at night. Each evening when the temperature cools below the bee's operating level, the females crawl into the nesting hole they have been working at. The children find it fascinating to wait until dark, and then visit the nesting holes with a flashlight, If you shine the light directly down the hole, your eye is greeted with a shiny black abdomen reflecting the light back to you.

It is not only great fun to count the bees, but it is valuable information for serious bee propagators. You can learn how many nesters you have, when their population peaks, and when they begin to die off — kind of a military muster of troop strength.

Children respond well to learning about these bees. The bees seem to stimulate that wonderful curiosity that children possess in such abundance. The secret to opening their minds to the wonder of nature is to make discovery fun. Use your Orchard Mason colony to catch a child's curiosity.

Let the children watch the bees emerge. Remember, most of the bees emerge from ten to eleven in the morning. You may find yourself having to explain about "the birds and the bees" but what better time and place? Don't make a big deal out of it. Treat the subject matter matter-of-factly and simply. The children will handle it just fine.

Observe together the insects feeding at a flowering shrub. As you look for your Orchard Masons you will see many other insects. Now you can point out the difference between flies and bees. Remember? Bees have four wings, flies but two. Bees have antennae, flies have none. You will see bumblebees and perhaps honeybees; tell them about the pollen baskets on bee's legs. You can watch the several varieties of bumblebees, forty-three separate species in North America, each with its own color pattern. Do the kids know that most bumbles nest in the ground, but that you can entice them to nest in a bumblebee house that you set out?

Explain pollination in a simple way and then go to see if you can find the Orchard Masons on the apple blossoms. Brush some pollen on the child's hand from a ripe blossom. Tell them about nectar and explain that bees drink it, partly to regurgitate it later to mix with their collected pollen.

Bee Collection

You might want to encourage a child to collect, identify and mount insects of a certain group. A collection of bees could be an exciting summer project for both a child or grandchild and yourself.

A beginning can be had by catching bees in a jar. A small flat paper box with plastic foam cut for the bottom will hold your collection. The small pins that come with new men's shirts are quite adequate for displaying your bees. Killing the insects may be the

most difficult part of the project. You can do this very efficiently by purchasing automotive starting fluid (ether) in a pressurized can. Any automotive store stocks ether because it is an extremely flammable gas. Sprayed into a reluctant carburetor, it will bring an engine roaring to life. It has the opposite effect on insects, and for that matter, on humans, so handle it with care.

A quick shot of ether under the lid of a quickly opened jar, will render the bees ready for display almost immediately. Pin the bees through the thorax, mount them on the foam bottom of your box, and begin the fun of identifying them.

If you allow the kids to participate at their own pace, they will share your pleasure in insects in general, and the Orchard Mason in particular. If you make the experience fun and interesting, you may kindle a lifelong appreciation for nature that will bring the child great satisfaction and joy. One never knows; you may inspire the twenty-first century's greatest naturalist.

Borrow a Microscope

If you have access to a reasonably good microscope, you are in for an afternoon of fun and wonderment. Put a dead Orchard Mason under the lens and focus on nature's incredible design. Now you can see the pollen carrying scopa for yourself. Look at the twin horns on the face of the female western Orchard Mason. If they point downward, you will be looking at her eastern cousin.

Can you see the delicate structure of the framework in her wings? Were you aware that bees have tiny hairs on their wings? Now check the bee over for mites. If she is carrying any, they will probably be clinging to hairs near where the wings connect to the thorax. Look for the true eyes, the three tiny smooth bumps on the forehead. Did you know that bees have two different kinds of eyes?

If you can find a bee that has just emerged with the red mites covering the thorax, get the bee under the microscope and look at that mass of mites. It may make your skin crawl, but it is fascinating.

I think nothing will so open the eyes of a child as their first look at the incredible architecture of an insect magnified. Be sure you give the children in your life the experience.

Use Your Imagination

There are many more interesting ways to exploit your experience with the Orchard Mason and to share its wonders with those around you. Enjoy your experience with this beneficial creature. I hope that you have shared my pleasure in learning about them, and that you will be inspired to introduce the Orchard Mason Bee to your back yard.

THE END

Eight Tips For Success With Orchard Mason Bees

- DO use 5/16-inch diameter nesting holes. A depth of 6 inches is ideal; shallower holes will work, but result in more male bees.

- DO use paper or wood nesting materials that can absorb some of the moisture from the food supply.

- DO place your nesting habitat on the wall of a building in the full sun. Place them under an eave to prevent rain from damaging the wood or paper.

- DO place your nesting habitat where it will get the most protection from cooling breezes.

- DO NOT place nesting habitat on fence posts, arbors or trees.

- DO NOT move nesting habitat during the bees' nesting season.

- DO move your nesting habitat into an unheated garage or outbuilding, or a refrigerator after mid September. You may move them into protection earlier if you move them gently. Store at 33 to 38 degrees if possible.

- DO hang your nesting habitat close together on the same wall. Remember, the bees are gregarious.

References

Buchmann, Stephen L. & Nabhan, Gary Paul, *The Forgotten Pollinators.* Island Press, Washington, DC., 1996.

Dickman, Greg, *Orchard Bees,* Auburn, Indiana.

Essig, E.O., *Insects of Western North America,* The MacMillan Co., 1926.

Krombein, Karl V., "Biological Notes on Chaetodactylus Krombeini Baker, A Parasitic Mite of the Megachilid Bee, Osmia lignaria Say." *Proc. Biological Society of Washington,* Vol. 75, pp 237-250.

Michener, Charles D., McGinley, Ronald J., & Danforth, Bryan N., *The Bee Genera of North and Central America.* Smithsonian Institution, 1994.

O'Toole, Christopher & Raw, Anthony, *Bees of The World,* Blandford Publishing, London. 1991.

Phillips, Joel K. & Klostermeyer, E.C., "Nesting behavior of Osmia lignaria propinqua Cresson." *Journal of the Kansas Entomological Society,* 51(1), pp 91-108, 1978.

Stephen, W. P., Bohart, G. E., & Torchio, P. F., *The Biology and External Morphology of Bees,* Agricultural Experiment Station, Oregon State University, 1969.

Torchio, Philip F., "Use of Osmia lignaria say as a pollinator in an apple and prune orchard," *Journal of the Kansas Entomological Society,* 49, pp 475-482, 1976.

Torchio, Philip F., "Use of Osmia lignaria propinqua as a mobile pollinator of orchard crops." *Environmental Entomology,* 20(2), pp 590-596, 1991.

Torchio, Philip F., "Field experiments with the pollinator species Osmia lignaria propinqua Cresson, in apple orchards." *Journal of the Kansas Entomological Society,* 58(3), pp 448-464, 1985.

Torchio, Philip F., *Use of non-honeybee species as pollinators of crops.* Entomological Society of Ontario, 118, pp 111-124, 1987.

Torchio, Philip F., "In-nest Biologies and Development of Immature Stages of Three Osmia Species." *Ann. Entomological Society of America,* 82(5), pp 599-615, 1989.

Torchio, Philip F., "Biology, Immature Development, and Adaptive Behavior of Stelis montana, A Cleptoparasite of Osmia." *Ann. Entomological Society of America,* 82(5), pp 616-632, 1989.

Torchio, Philip F., "Effects of Spore Dosage and Temperature on Pathogenic Expressions of Chalkbrood Syndrome Caused by Ascophaera Torchioi Within Larvae of Osmia lignaria propinqua." *Environmental Entomology,* 21(5), pp 1086-1091, 1992.

Torchio, Philip J. & Bosch, J., "Biology of Tricrania Stansburyi, a Meloid Beetle Cleptoparasite of the Bee Osmia lignaria propinqua (Hymenoptera: Megachilidae)." *Ann. Entomological Society of America,* 85(6), pp 713-721, 1992.

Torchio, Philip F., Personal correspondence since 1992.

United States Department of Agriculture. *Insects, the Yearbook of Agriculture.* 1952.

Washington State University. *Orchard Mason Bee.* Extension Service Bulletin 0922. July 1981.

The Xerces Society, *"Wings,"* Fall vol., pp 4-13, 1991.

Observation Notes

START YOUR OWN
ORCHARD MASON BEE COLONY

You can buy a starting population of Orchard Mason Bees and the related items described in this book from selected garden centers and nature stores across the country.

Contact Knox Cellars for a list of our dealers near your home, or for our mail-order catalog, if you do not have a Knox Cellars dealer nearby.

Knox Cellars Native Bee Products

- Orchard Mason Bees in paper liners
- Orchard Mason Bees in wooden slices
- "System" nesting tubes
- "System Nester"
- "Nester Liners"
- Nester Shelter
- Shelter Extensions
- Wooden nesting blocks for three types of native bees
- "The Gift of Pollination"
- "Build a Bee House" kit
- *Humblebee Bumblebee*, by Brian Griffin
- *The Orchard Mason Bee*, by Brian Griffin
- *Bees of the World,* by O'Toole & Raw
- Video, *The Orchard Mason Bee*
- Audio cassette *The Orchard Mason Bee*
- "Humble Bumble Home," bumblebee nest box
- Bumblebee tee shirts
- Orchard Mason Bee tee shirts

Knox Cellars Native Bee Pollinators

1607 Knox Ave.
Bellingham, WA 98225
Tel: (360) 733-3283
Fax: (360) 733-3283
Email: brian@knoxcellars.com

25724 NE 10th St.
Redmond WA 98053
Tel: (425) 898-8802
Fax: (425) 898-8070
Email: lisa@knoxcellars.com

Please visit our website: www.knoxcellars.com